Making War in the Heavenlies

A Different Look at Spiritual Warfare

By
Bill Randles

Acknowledgements

Extracts from the Authorized Version of the Bible (The King James Bible), the rights in which are vested in the Crown, are reproduced by permission of the Crown's patentee, Cambridge University Press.

First published in the USA 1994

All rights reserved. No part of this publication may be reproduced, stored in a retrieval system, or transmitted, in any form or by any means, electronic, mechanical, photocopying recording or otherwise without the prior permission in writing of the Copyright owner.

ISBN: 978-0-9646626-0-5

Front picture by Bob North Jnr.

Table of Contents

Introduction: My Story	7

PART 1

Chapter One: An Overall View of the Problem of Spiritual Warfare	**11**
Dominionism: What is it?	14
Mysticism	15
Anti-Criticism	18
False Eschatology	19
Chapter One Endnotes	*20*
Chapter Two: More Basic Beliefs and Basic Errors	**21**
True Warfare	23
Territorial Spirits	25
God Appointed the Spiritual Rulers	27
The Church Without Spot or Wrinkle?	29
"If the Church Would Only Do Its Job"	30
Chapter Two Endnotes	*32*
Chapter Three: Man-Centered or God-Centered?	**33**
The Dominion of Christ Over His Enemies	34
An Old View of Victory	35
Easy Believism	37
Did the Apostles Practise It?	38
Chapter Three Endnotes	*39*
Chapter Four: A Warning To Charismatics	**40**
Other Misconceptions	41
Choose Your Battles – Are we Fighting the Right Enemy?	42
Attacking Your City	43
Two Principles at Work	45
Chapter Four Endnotes	*46*

Chapter Five: Presumptuous Are They! — 47
- Railing Accusations — 49
- The Church as Scapegoat — 53
- Rejection of the Rapture — 54
- False Confirmation — 56
- The Real Problem — 57
- Five Criteria By Which To Judge — 59
- Receiving the Love of the Truth — 61
- *Chapter Five Endnotes* — *63*

PART 2
Chapter Six: What Is True Spiritual Warfare? — 64
- The Scriptural Use of Spiritual Warfare — 64
- The Sovereignty of God — 66
- The Early Church Worshipped a Despot — 67
- God Is Still The Sovereign Lord of History — 70
- What It Means to Worship the Sovereign God — 73

Chapter Seven: Your Adversary And His Strategy — 79
- Keep To Your Boundaries — 79
- How Does The Kingdom of God Come? — 89
- Deception – What Is It? — 90
- Everything must be tested by the Word! — 95

Chapter Eight: A Case History of True Warfare — 100
- A Case Study of Spiritual Warfare — 100
- Conclusion — 106

Appendix One: Rodney Howard-Browne:
An Analysis of the Laughing Revival — 109
- The Issue of Sensuality — 111
- The Issue of Reverence — 115
- The Bias Against Truth — 117
- Repentance — 120
- Beware — 121
- *Appendix One References* — *122*

Appendix Two: Spiritual Warfare – Quo Vadis?   **123**
Replacement Theology   124
Presumptuous?   127
The Deceptive Counterfeit   128
Appendix Two References   *129*

Appendix Three: Spiritual Warfare And Evangelism   **130**
Questions   130
1. What is the true aim of today's "Evangelism"?......   131
Healing The Land – A Quest For Kingdom Now   131
Spiritual Warfare   133
The Kingdom Factor   136
Uniting For The Kingdom   137
Networking   141
2. Does the Bible indicate a global revival before the return of Christ?   142
The Way to Calvary   143
Endtimes Prophecy   144
3. What is the "gospel" preached at modern day evangelistic events?   145
4. What is biblical evangelism?   148
What then shall we do?   150
Appendix Three References   *152*

Appendix Four:
Gnosticism: What is it?   153
History and Definition   153
What is This Gnosis?   154
The Gnostic Obsession with Self   156
Gnosticism is Highly Individualized   157
Elitism   159
Dualism   161
John's Remedy for Gnosticism   163
A Return to True Humanity   166
Gnostic Distortions of Christ's Person   166
Another Gnostic Distortion of Christ   169
Is There a Remedy for Gnosticism?   170
Appendix Four References   *176*

Introduction

My Story

My name is Bill Randles, and I am a Christian. I have been a follower of Christ for seventeen years. I am a Pastor in the city of Cedar Rapids, Iowa. I have a wife, Kris, and four children, two girls and two boys. Our Church has been in existence for twelve years. It is called Believers in Grace Fellowship and we are a united, loving community. I was saved in the fall of 1977 in an Assembly of God church. I answered the altar call about thirty different times seeking the assurance of my salvation. One night I was quite depressed, not having found the security of Faith in Christ but striving for it for quite some time. In my despondency, I picked up a Bible and began reading II Corinthians 5, just a chapter I picked at random. Reading with a distracted mind, I soon realized I had re-read the chapter about ten times, when all at once verse 21 was illuminated to me by the Holy Ghost!

***II Corinthians 5:21** For he hath made him to be sin for us, who knew no sin; that we might be made the righteousness of God in him.*

He had taken my place. He was made sin for me, that I might receive His righteousness. Hallelujah! It is hard to explain, but I hope many who read this book will know what I am talking about. The received assurance of peace with God. II Corinthians 5:21, and Romans 8:1-3, were real to me and I entered into the promised rest. Through many years, toils and snares, tears and victories, our Lord has been able to keep me from stumbling (utterly). I trust He will preserve me blameless until His coming and He will make me to stand with joy before our God and Father.

In the Assembly of God in which I was saved, which was a loving community of faith, one of the members had slipped me a twelve-pack of Kenneth Copeland tapes. I devoured them immediately. You could say, for the next three to five years, I cut my teeth on the teachings of Kenneth Copeland. Gradually, I absorbed the full spectrum of what has been called the Word Movement or the Faith Movement lead by Fred Price, Kenneth Hagin, Jerry Savelle, and others. I am sure there were many positive things imparted to me, but I got to the point in my life where I just couldn't continue in that vein. One of the most appalling and glaring contradictions I observed was the "little gods" teaching – the idea that we are in God's class of being, little gods in God's exact likeness and image, and so forth. I knew this was the exact lie of Satan in the Garden, but this is what much of the Faith message promoted, spawned by the heretical teaching of E. W. Kenyon.

Over the years, I have been around the Faith people and have noticed a progression. The process seems to have began with faith; faith as a force – a metaphysical view of faith, instead of biblical faith with moral content. Faith as spiritual law, making no moral demands. It "works" equally for the unrighteous as well as the righteous. This is faith in faith itself!

From faith and confidence, the stream carries us to "our dominion and authority." The main goal is to find out who you are in Christ and to realize your potential in your authority in Christ. We are led to believe that reigning as kings in this life is the whole goal of Christianity.

This stream now flows together with another errant stream in the Body – the Reconstructionists, who also believe in a kind of Christian dominion. The flowing together of these two – the evangelical, political dominionists and the charismatic, faith, spiritual power dominionists – has largely determined the agenda of the "Religious-Right," Moral Majority Movement of the 80's and 90's. Where is this progression leading us and is it based on sound premises? What is the call of the Church? To what does the Great Commission refer? These are subjects worthy of our attention. I am only addressing a portion of this subject in this writing.

The next step in the progression takes us from metaphysical faith, through dominion and authority, on into spiritual warfare. There are other phases of this "flow." The restoration of the "fivefold ministry" is being emphasized: apostles, prophets, evangelists, pastors and teachers. The restoration of prophets, in particular, seems to be of great interest in Charismatic circles lately.

This is a matter of concern to me and I hope and pray to God it will be to many others also. I am taking a two-pronged approach. First, I offer criticism of the current concepts being presented and popularly accepted today in the name of spiritual warfare. All I ask you to do is to be a "Berean."

Acts 17:11 *These* [Bereans] *were more noble than those in Thessalonica, in that they received the word with all readiness of mind, and searched the scriptures daily, whether those things were so.*

Secondly, I will set forth, in brief fashion, an introduction to the biblical teaching of the believer's warfare.

We live in perilous times. People are not necessarily hungry for God and the love of the cross, but they are hungry for the supernatural. This is not a good development. Often times people want the things of God without submission to the will of God. A kind of cross-less Christianity has been set forth. May we receive the love of the truth before it is too late!

It's not that people are enemies of Christ. They have become enemies of the cross of Christ, which puts man in his place before God. We are not gods nor are we on God's plane or in God's class. We are sinners – redeemed yes – but sinners. Glory be to God for His matchless mercy and indescribable grace! There is no substitute for sound doctrine to help correct this tendency towards error that we all have. My prayer is that this writing will carry the anointing of the Spirit and the truth that can set us free!

Bill Randles

Part One

1

An Overall View of the Problem of Spiritual Warfare

Romans 10:2 *For I bear them record that they have a zeal of God, but not according to knowledge.*

To open this discussion, I would like to lay out a sampling of what many consider to be a disturbing trend in the Body of Christ, namely the trend toward militant, spiritualised, mystical warfare.

The following quotations, anecdotes, and excerpts all underscore the fact that the church, particularly the Charismatic, evangelical church, is drifting into an agenda radically different from the one the Lord and the Apostles held to. The following is a kind of "menu of error," a smorgasbord of zeal indeed, but not according to knowledge. It is not my intention to accuse, or cast anyone in a bad light, although I feel we must be very specific. I assume that the men and women whom we discuss are truly committed servants of Christ. I believe it is vital that we be able to discuss public teaching, publicly, without taking personal offence.

- Item 1 Argentina. Christian leaders openly challenge, mock, taunt, and curse Satan and Evil Spirits.[1]
- Item 2 San Jose, California. After "seasoned veterans" of spiritual warfare met to discuss how to "purge the skies" over the actual locations (geographical) of two "strongmen," 900 prayer warriors fanned out with a special decree. They climbed to mountain tops, top floor rooms of hotels, and even the tops of tall

buildings. At the agreed upon hour, they broke the seals off their proclamation and jointly declared, "To the Dark Powers over San Jose and the surrounding communities, that we are taking back our land in Jesus' name!"[2]

- Item 3 This is an excerpt from an article in the **Los Angeles Times**, February 17, 1990 by John Dart. Headline "Evangelicals and Charismatics Prepare for Spiritual Warfare."

> **Growing numbers of evangelical and Charismatic Christian leaders are preparing broad assaults on what they call the cosmic powers of darkness.**
>
> **Fascinated with the notion that Satan commands a hierarchy of territorial demons, some mission agencies and big church pastors are devising strategies for "breaking the strongholds" of those evil spirits alleged to be controlling cities and countries. Some proponents in the fledgling movement already maintain that focused prayer meetings have ended the curse of the Bermuda Triangle, led to the 1987 downfall in Oregon of free love guru Baghwhan Shree Rajneesh, and for the 1984 Summer Olympics in Los Angeles, produced a two week drop in the crime rate, a friendly atmosphere, and unclogged freeways.**[3]

- Item 4 Sweden.

> **In order to spy on a society in Sweden that is attempting to revive the ancient religion of the Vikings and is worshipping the Asa-gods, this same Christian spy-intercessor became a member of the Society. Of course, he did not use his real name. On his door he had two interchangeable nameplates. He is always well informed about the activities of New Age groups and Satanists and he has a nose to track down the information that prayer warriors need.**[4]

- Item 5 **Charisma Magazine** advertisement for evangelist Wayne Parks. "Wayne Parks is coming, and the Devil is running." **Charisma**, June 1993, page 9. Another ad for a conference shows pictures of the speakers, and then in bold letters, "Holy Spirit Explosion,"

> Come and join with these men of divine destiny as we wage "Holy War" against the kingdom of darkness...God said it's

time to sound the trumpet of battle and take Miami back from the clutches of the Devil!"

- Item 6 Have you ever heard of Spiritual Mapping? You say you don't even know what it is? Get with it! It is a new technique considered a "must do" for taking your city for God! Spiritual mapping involves researching the secular and religious history of a city to determine the names and characteristics of "ruling spirits" over the area. In spiritual warfare knowing the name of the strongman is a must. If you are really right on, you can actually determine the address; the geographical location of the spirit! According to Dick Bernal, the way to take a city is fourfold.

1. Proclaim a fast with prayer.
2. Identify the principality over the city.
3. Determine its geographical location.
4. Call him/her by name.5

Bernal also tells us that God revealed to him the name of the ruling principality over his city. "In prayer, the Holy Spirit impressed upon me that the title of the ruling principality over our area is; "Self.""[6] (I didn't know that self was an evil spirit, what a relief, that lets me off the hook).

- Item 7 Earl Paulk. "Christ in us must take dominion over the earth...the next move of God cannot occur until Christ in us takes dominion."[7]

I could go on and on, but I think this sampler has made the point. Something seriously wrong is flourishing here. The Pentecostal, Charismatic, and some of the Evangelical Church have a new attitude. We are "mighty warriors" now. We don't have to be wimps, we now "serve Satan notice" we are taking back our cities. Even our worship services are more like military pep rallies, with more emphasis on making war in the heavenlies and tearing down principalities, than the "Old Rugged Cross," or "I Surrender All." Kind of reminds me of the crusades, zealous, yes, but severely misguided and based on false premises. I believe that unless we are checked on this one, many are going to be in for severe disillusionment and hurt. Allow me please to articulate the false premises that I believe are undergirding this concept of spiritual warfare.

Dominionism: What is it?

There has developed a general consensus among Charismatics about the role of the Christian, as to what "Ruling and Reigning" with Christ means. As I said in the introduction, I was "raised" up as a young Christian in the teachings of the Faith Movement. One particularly attractive teaching, to me, was the doctrine of the fall of ADAM. I summarize it this way. I believed with millions of others:

I. God created ADAM to have dominion over the earth. Adam was "god of this world."

II. ADAM handed that dominion over to Satan, who is now "god of this world," and God couldn't do anything about it.

III. Jesus came to restore that dominion back to us.

IV. Through Jesus, Christians have a mandate to "take dominion" over all of this earth and rule over all earthly institutions.

V. In the Last Days there will be a company of Christians who, knowing who they are in Christ and what they possess, in Him, will display the supernatural power of God and usher in a Last Days Revival!

VI. Finally, Jesus will come and receive from us the kingdom and He will rule and reign.

The problem with Dominionism, is that it is man-centered. We will "take dominion," be the victorious army. We are the "violent ones" who will take the kingdom by force. In fact, our view exalts us over all previous generations of Christians, The Last Days "Manchild." As Rick Joyner prophesied in **The Harvest,**

> **In the near future the church will not be looking back at the First Century church with envy because of the great exploits of those days, but all will be saying that He certainly did save the best wine for last...You who have dreamed of one day being able to talk with Peter,**

John, and Paul are going to be surprised to find that they have all been waiting to talk to you![8]

Doesn't that just make you feel great? The dominion teaching exalts man, singing about how "We are more than conquerors," (forgetting it is, "through Him who gave himself for us"). In Dominion thinking the idea is to learn "who we are in Christ," our rights and privileges and authority. The examples of spiritual warfare testimonies at the beginning of the chapter are merely examples of people "taking dominion" to its logical conclusion.

To a "dominion" minded person, the Great Commission of Matthew 28:18 and Genesis 1:26 are interchangeable. God gave us a mandate to control all of this earth and we have the authority to do it! The idea is, "If the church would do her job, there wouldn't be all this crime, suffering and rebellion. If we had just known our authority in Christ..." The end result is to make the church responsible for the suffering of the unbeliever.

Mysticism

Mysticism is another faulty premise on which much of spurious spiritual warfare is based. Mysticism is the exaltation of subjective experience over objective truth. "God showed me the name of the strongman, "Self." " How can I argue with that? God showed it to you, it's not open to discussion, right? Not unless you make the decision to submit every subjective experience to the Truth of the Word of God, which is objective. (Subjective means it happened to me, I felt, saw it or heard it! Objective means outside of me, independent of my experience. The Resurrection of Jesus happened in history, whether you "felt it" or not).

Mysticism flourishes now because of the unbiblical bias against truth in the church today. That's right. The church has become biased against objective truth! How many times have you heard the plea for us to get rid of our "silly doctrine," and come together in unity? Doctrine has become a dirty word in some circles. What is doctrine? It is the body of objective truth, the teaching of God's Word. Doctrine is the only basis for evaluating spiritual experience.

This is why Satan wants to move us away from it. Without doctrine, all you have to judge by, are your own fickle feelings. If it feels right it must be right! Or, if it "works" it's right. When you hear Christian TV personalities or musicians railing against "those heresy hunters," or a third wave "prophet" warning against Jezebel, or a fault finding spirit, you are hearing the hiss of the Serpent! The Charismatic churches desperately need critical thinking at every level, even if they don't like the packaging it comes in. Anything that is truly of God can endure the most intense scrutiny.

Psalm 12:6 The words of the Lord are pure words: as silver tried in a furnace of earth, purified seven times.

Here are some examples of mysticism. The many detailed descriptions of "strongmen" over cities and how they operate, could only have been "revealed" mystically because there is no such description in the Word of God. I have a friend, an advocate of the Spiritual Warfare Movement and author, whose books are widely read as an author. This friend told me the "Jezebel" spirit came to him in the night to try to bargain with him to quit exposing her through preaching. He has constant dreams, visions, and revelations in which either the Lord or agents from the other side, "come to him." All of this is sheer mysticism, the non-biblical, experiential method of attaining to spiritual truth and progress. Did the Apostles have such experiences? Did they describe "strongmen," or research city histories to try to discern the strongman? Obviously, not. So much of this, "The Lord told me..." goes unchallenged today! Every dream, vision, and prophecy ought to be so closely scrutinized and cross-examined that anyone would think long and hard before even whispering, "Thus saith the Lord..." Only then will we see a restoration of truly spiritual gifts.

This flood of extra-biblical, mystical revelation is conditioning the church to accept anything from any source. Dick Bernal in **Storming Hell's Brazen Gates**, devotes several pages of illustrations and at least one chapter to Greek and Roman mythology. C. Peter Wagner in his book, **The Third Wave of the**

Holy Spirit, makes one of his points from the Apocryphal Books, the Acts of Peter and the Acts of John.[9] In the Acts of Peter, Wagner finds support for a

> **spiritual shootout after a great deal of braggadocio and confrontational theatrics. All this involved manhandling them [demons], making them howl, beg for mercy, tell their secrets and depart in a hurry.**

From the Acts of John, he tells the story of John's "Power Encounter" in Ephesus, at the Temple of Artemis, which split in pieces after John prayed. Why do we need to learn about spiritual warfare through pagan mythology, or the gnostic, non-inspired Apocrypha? Could it be that the doctrine doesn't have enough support from the Holy Scripture itself? The Spiritual Warfare Movement is rampantly mystical. Personal experience is held on a par with scripture. Dreams, visions, and revelations often outweigh scripture. God, so it seems, has to give us extra-biblical Revelation; special teaching that the Apostles knew nothing of, because we are the last days, cutting edge overcomers! We are about to do, supposedly, what no church has ever done before, cleanse the heavenlies of evil spirits and establish the kingdom, ushering in the millennium!

Isaiah 8:20 To the law and to the testimony: if they speak not according to this word, it is because there is no light in them.

II Timothy 4:3-4 For the time will come when they will not endure sound doctrine; but after their own lusts shall they heap to themselves teachers, having itching ears; And they shall turn away their ears from the truth, and shall be turned unto fables.

Anti-Criticism

What are we to think of the "prophet" who emphatically told us that on Thursday, June 9, "All evil would be ripped off the face of the earth?" He certainly prophesied on an open forum, Trinity Broadcasting Network! Has he been censured, rebuked, or even mildly denounced? There is a twofold result of this ungodly rejection of critical thinking. One, those outside the Pentecostal world can't give us any credibility, consequently they can't receive our gospel. Especially those who, though unsaved, are intellectually honest. The other result is even more frightening. Those in the Charismatic, Pentecostal world, are either growing cynical and disillusioned, or they are being conditioned to the point of not having a conscience. "Judge not..." or "Touch not my anointed..." and countless other half scriptures are being used to deflect valid criticism. Especially in the Warfare Movement is this prominent. The teaching about "The Accuser," or "Jezebel," or "fault finding spirits," are an effective safeguard against the Berean attitude. How? Well, we know that Jezebel persecuted the true prophets, therefore what spirit do you have, if you question these humble servants? Bingo! You have a Jezebel spirit! (You're catching on!)

Lack of unity is being presented as the one great hindrance to the great Last Days Revival, and consequently, the coming of the Lord. But, is lack of unity warned about as much as lack of truth, as a last days danger? I think not. Nor is a lack of signs and wonders warned of, in fact, signs and wonders will be abundant in those days.

II Thessalonians 2:9-12 Even him, whose coming is after the working of Satan with all power and signs and lying wonders, and with all deceivableness of unrighteousness in them that perish; because they received not the love of the truth, that they might be saved. And for this cause God shall send them strong delusion, that they should believe a lie: That they might be damned who believed not the truth, but had pleasure in unrighteousness.

It's the whole issue of "truth" that we are warned to safeguard. But the present "ideal" will be fulfilled when we "throw out all of our silly doctrines and come together across denominational lines, Catholic, Baptist, Charismatic, Methodist, and any who call on Jesus as Lord!" The erroneous idea is that love, not truth is the basis for unity. This is the kind of thinking that is paving the way for the Harlot, Superchurch of the Last Days. And the Spiritual Warfare Movement with its call for a city-wide all inclusive church and it's ecumenical Jesus marches, is highly motivated by that very agenda. It's still man-centered. "Jesus is waiting for us to come together before He will return, we have to get it together." We have actually misinterpreted Psalm 110 to mean that it is us, not the Lord who will make Jesus' enemies His footstool!

Psalm 110:1 *The Lord said unto my Lord, Sit thou at my right hand, until I make thine enemies thy footstool.*

Who wants to speak out against love and unity? I don't. But, can you truly divorce love from truth?

False Eschatology

Spiritual warfare is built on a false eschatology.

II Peter 3:3-4 *Knowing this first, that there shall come in the last days scoffers, walking after their own lusts, and saying, Where is the promise of his coming? For since the fathers fell asleep, all things continue as they were from the beginning of the creation.*

The trend began to develop in the early 1980's, that is, the trend of scoffing at the Rapture, as "the escape theory."

Luke 21:36 *Watch ye therefore, and pray always, that ye may be accounted worthy to escape all these things that shall come to pass, and to stand before the Son of man.*

Many confess having a problem with Rapture teaching, for in their judgement it isn't sufficiently optimistic. Scriptures that teach,

Evil men and seducers will wax worse and worse... or *In the last days perilous times will come...* and *Will the Son of Man find faith when He comes to the earth?* evidently aren't optimistic enough. After all, where is the victory? The great end time revival that shakes nations? A more optimistic eschatology has been "revealed" in which we won't need to be "rescued from the evils of this present age." We will be too busy ruling the nations!

This is what happens when men try to subject God's plan to their own opinions about what victory and defeat mean. To Peter, the cross Jesus warned of was much too pessimistic, a theology of defeat! *Not so, Lord.* We have to be careful of savouring the things that be of men over the things of God.

Chapter One Endnotes

1. Wagner, C. Peter & 17 Veterans of Spiritual Warfare. **Engaging the Enemy**. Regal Books. Page 46.
2. Bernal, Dick. **Storming Hell's Brazen Gates through Militant, Violent, Prevailing Prayer.** Jubilee Christian Center. Page 65.
3. Dart, John. "Evangelicals and Charismatics Prepare for Spiritual Warfare." Los Angeles Times. 17 Feb 1990. Page F16.
4. Sjoberg, Kjell. **Breaking Strongholds in Your City.** Chapter 4, "Spiritual Mapping for Prophetic Prayer Action." Regal Books. Page 99.
5. Bernal, Dick. Page 55.
6. Bernal, Dick. Page 30.
7. Paulk, Earl. **Held in the Heavens Until.**
8. Joyner, Rick. **The Harvest.** Whitaker House. Page 26.
9. Wagner, C. Peter. **The Third Wave of the Holy Spirit.** Vine Books. Pages 80-81.

2

More Basic Beliefs and Basic Errors

There truly is SPIRITUAL WARFARE! I do not to deny the reality of it, rather I intend to sharpen our current understanding of spiritual warfare and to challenge errant beliefs on the subject in our day.

Ephesians 6:10-18 Finally, my brethren, be strong in the Lord, and in the power of his might. Put on the whole armour of God, that ye may be able to stand against the wiles of the devil. For we wrestle not against flesh and blood, but against principalities, against powers, against the rulers of the darkness of the world, against spiritual wickedness in high places. Wherefore take unto you the whole armour of God, that ye may be able to withstand in the evil day, and having done all, to stand. Stand therefore, having your loins girt about with truth, and having on the breastplate of righteousness; And your feet shod with the preparation of the gospel of peace; Above all, taking the shield of faith, wherewith ye shall be able to quench all the fiery darts of the wicked. And take the helmet of salvation, and the sword of the Spirit, which is the word of God; Praying always with all prayer and supplication in the Spirit, and watching thereunto with all perseverance and supplication for all saints.

In this passage the apostle is teaching the Church to be aware of the unseen hosts arrayed against it, and show us the spiritual and moral equipment with which to arm itself. And having done all, we are to stand (literally withstand, stand against). That is to be our spiritual posture in this warfare: armoured with the Spiritual Armour – holding up the Spiritual Shield, wielding the Spiritual Sword – we are to withstand.

But, people in the current Spiritual Warfare Movement have taken this concept a step further than the idea of being armed with the armour of God, standing in prayer and intercession for the people of God, and wielding the sword of the Spirit. They have gone beyond preaching the Gospel to a wicked and perverted generation. Through misapplication of these truths the Church has moved into a fleshly militancy. They are now on the attack against Satan.

To explain my objections, allow me to outline the basic beliefs of much of the Spiritual Warfare Movement, and to raise a few issues. If you will be Bereans – searching the scriptures for yourselves – then you will see if these things be so.

One major belief is based on a misapplication of II Corinthians 10:3-5.

For though we walk in the flesh, we do not war after the flesh. For the weapons of our warfare are not carnal, but mighty through God to the pulling down of strongholds; Casting down imaginations, and every high thing that exalted itself against the knowledge of God, and bringing into captivity every thought to the obedience of Christ.

Spiritual warfare, the apostle is teaching, is not carnal but spiritual, mighty, and powerful. He even tells us in this chapter where the warfare is located. Spiritual warfare is located in the minds of men. The strongholds are patterns of thinking, that allow men to "hold out" against God's Gospel. A thought becomes a knowledge (against the knowledge of God), this knowledge becomes an imagination, which develops into a stronghold, all designed to alienate from God. All of the battle is in the minds of men, their patterns of thinking.

However, the new idea (maybe not new! Gnostics believed very similarly in the first, second, and third centuries) is that strongholds are located over cities (literally) in the heavenly places (ie. in the sky)! The teaching is that there are Satanic strongholds over individuals, families, nations, and so on. The idea of modern spiritual warfare is to bombard these strongholds through focused prayer, bringing them down. To make a direct attack on Satan and his minions.

Now, I will be the first to admit that prayer, agonized pleading, and intercession to God for the vitality of the Church, the salvation of sinners, and the in-gathering of the lost, is truly the need of the hour! Who wants to come against prayer? But, "Warfare" prayer is primarily focused on Satan and evil spirits located in the sky over specific cities. This, it seems to me, is missing the true focus. It's like the bull is attacking the red cloth instead of the matador! To be reoriented to God's purpose need to return to a correct understanding of II Corinthians 10:3-5.

Our struggle is to overthrow the erroneous patterns of thinking that keep people blinded to the Gospel.

True Warfare

II Corinthians 4:3-4 But if our Gospel be hid, it is hid to them that are lost: In whom the god of this world hath blinded the minds of them which believe not, lest the light of the glorious Gospel of Christ, who is the image of God, should shine unto them.

Our spiritual weapons are prayer and preaching – prayer for souls, revival, Holy Ghost conviction. We need biblical weapons, such as preaching that confronts and demolishes the vain imaginations, and the high things that exalt themselves against the knowledge of God. Spiritual warfare is stripping away man's fig leaf of self-righteousness. Through our anointed preaching, the Holy Spirit destroys the refuge of lies, the self-justification, idolatry, humanism, and psychology that opposes the truth. Lovingly, but systematically, we destroy these reasonings through divine arguments. Frankly, sometimes I'd rather pray against citywide "strongholds" than confront people with their false belief systems – it's easier!

Let's look at a biblical example of spiritual warfare. In Acts 17 we see the Apostle Paul engaged in spiritual warfare.

Acts 17:1-3 *Now when they had passed through Amphipolis and Apollonia, they came to Thessalonica, where was a synagogue of the Jews; and Paul, as his manner was, went in unto them, and three sabbath days reasoned with them out of the scriptures, opening and alleging, that Christ must needs have suffered, and risen again from the dead; and that this Jesus, whom I preach unto you, is Christ.*

Note Paul's spiritual warfare, which consists of: reasoning, debating, opening, and alleging. Why? Was Paul just contentious? (Hung up on doctrine?) No. He knew that before the Thessalonians could be saved, their vain imaginations, reasonings, and high thoughts that exalted themselves against the knowledge of God had to be challenged and destroyed.

Acts 17:16-18 *Now while Paul waited for them at Athens, his spirit was stirred in him, when he saw the city wholly given to idolatry. Therefore disputed he in the synagogue with the Jews, and with the devout persons, and in the market daily with them that met with them. Then certain philosophers of the Epicureans, and of the Stoics, encountered him. And some said, what will this babbler say? Others said, He seemeth to be a setter forth of strange gods; because he preached unto them Jesus, and the resurrection.*

A whole city was given to idolatry! That will stir anyone who loves Jesus! I will say this about many proponents of the Spiritual Warfare Movement: they are concerned about some valid things. We really do need revival and a move of the Spirit. That's what we all want. They are concerned also about the salvation of souls, as we are. But, when Paul's spirit was stirred in Athens, because of the gross idolatry, he didn't wage spiritual warfare against Zeus or Apollo. In fact, he didn't name any spirit, tear down any principalities or any such thing. Paul waged spiritual warfare by "disputing in the synagogue with the Jews, and with the devout persons, and in the market daily, with them that met with him." (Verse 17)

The warfare intensified when "certain philosophers of the Epicureans and the Stoics encountered him..." (Acts 17:18). Now here we have spiritual warfare! Out in the marketplace of ideas, Paul was promoting the doctrine of Christ, setting Christ forth in the face of Epicureanism, Stoicism, Platonism, and all the philosophies of the day which Satan was using to darken men's minds. It is patterns of thinking that need to be directly confronted, philosophies that exalt themselves against the knowledge of God!

While Christians are waging phoney war against Jezebel, lust and other "strongmen," humanism, psychology, selfism, and so on are going unchallenged, and are even being promoted in our churches! When Paul waged war in Athens, his spiritual warfare consisted of the ideas of men being confronted by the Gospel of God! I will go through the sermon of Acts 17 at a later point in this writing. Its salient points are a great primer of the actual lines of battle we should be waging. But, first turn to Daniel 10.

Territorial Spirits

Spiritual warfare proponents are using scripture, but they are misapplying it. Here is an example of this. Daniel 10:12-13 is commonly used as a proof text.

***Daniel 10:12-13** Then said he unto me, Fear not, Daniel; for from the first day that thou didst set thine heart to understand and to chasten thyself before thy God, thy words were heard, and I am come for thy words. But, the prince of the kingdom of Persia withstood me one and twenty days; but, lo, Michael, one of the chief princes, came to help me; and I remained there with the kings of Persia. Daniel 10:20 Then said he, Knowest thou wherefore I come* *unto thee? and now will I return to fight with the prince of Persia; and when I am gone forth, lo, the prince of Grecia shall come.*

From these texts we get the idea of territorial spirits. I don't deny the possible reality of territorial spirits, but I would also add that we only know as much as is revealed about these matters.

Deuteronomy 29:29 *The secret things belong unto the Lord our God; but those things which are revealed belong unto us and to our children for ever, that we may do all the words of this law.*

Whatever we need to know, God has revealed in the scripture. But, when spiritual warfare proponents teach that over every area there is a spirit, a principality, a power, or an entity, that we are to bring down, I submit to you that this is beyond scripture. To believe in their existence is one thing, but what to do about them is another. Did God say we can "bring down principalities over cities?" (I hate to start any sentence with "Did God say," if you know what I mean). We are told to tear down vain imaginations and high thinking, bringing thoughts into captivity.

All of this has to do with men's minds. Please allow me to make three observations about this text.

1. Yes, this text implies that there are some kinds of territorial spirits: the prince of Persia withstands the angel; Daniel's prayers are hindered from being answered; Michael has to assist the angel. We are told of a Prince of Grecia, replacing the Prince of Persia. Wow! These are things hard to understand, but I accept them.

2. In all those days of prayer, we don't read once of Daniel addressing the prince of Persia, such as, "You prince of Persia, come down! I bring down that stronghold over Persia." Now, having been around spiritual warfare circles, I can say that that kind of prayer is fairly common place. In many cases, intercessory prayer has become more focused on Satan than on God. Even many worship services are focused more on "bringing down principalities, and making war in the heavenlies" than "How Great Thou Art". This is a sad thing. This is the unfortunate result of a misguided militancy in the Church. I even know of a "worship" song called "Only the Strong Survive!". Preposterous!

3. When the prince of Persia was displaced, he was only replaced by the prince of Greece – an even worse spirit in many respects. (Not many are deceived by Persian philosophy, but millions are by Greek philosophy). Think about it! When this "prince" was unseated, the vacuum was quickly filled by another strongman.

Could it be that when people bind strongmen in the powerful name of Jesus, a worse spirit comes along? I don't know, but it is something to think about.

For example, are Los Angeles, San Francisco, or Miami any better off since the late 80's early 90's when there were warfare prayer conferences in each city, directed against specific principalities? Or are they now worse off? Show me one city that is "cleansed of demonic activity" by spiritual warfare. Their claims are nonsense! However, Jesus did teach about unclean spirits being driven out and then returning to the clean, empty house with seven worse spirits. (Matthew 12:43-45). We are trafficking in things we don't understand, powerful things which are out of our league.

God Appointed the Spiritual Rulers

Do you believe in the sovereignty of God? Is it up to us to "cleanse the heavenlies" or is God in control? Power belongs to God:

Psalm 62:11-12 God hath spoken once; twice have I heard this; that power belongeth unto God. Also unto thee, O Lord, belongeth mercy; for thou renderest to every man according to his work.

God brings down and God exalts. If God had no use for Satan and his hierarchy – he would have fried them centuries ago! In His counsel and good pleasure, he has chosen to allow a hierarchy of demonic principalities over the nations of this world. We have to remember that God has called Satan the prince of this world. He has allowed Satan to blind the eyes of those who believe not. I don't understand God's ways in appointing these spiritual rulers (of the darkness of this age), but I accept it. And I'm not living in fear of them, either. The Bible calls these evil powers non-entities! They are "nothings!"

1 Cor 8:4-7 We know that an idol is nothing in the world, and that there is none other God but one. For though there be that are called gods, whether in heaven or in earth, (as there be gods many, and lords many,) But to us there is but one God, the Father, of whom are all things, and we in him; and one Lord Jesus Christ, by whom are all things, and we by him.

I Chron 16:26 For all the gods of the people are idols [Hebrew אלילים = ELILIM, nothings, vanities, non-entities]: *but the LORD made the heavens.*

Since God created all things, including the heavenlies and the angels, both good and bad, He is in control of them. He already has a plan to deal with the fallen spiritual rulers! And the plan doesn't involve the Church doing spiritual warfare to help God out.

The early believers had an attitude towards principalities and powers – not aggressive, militant warfare to pull them down, but confidence that God had set the Church in a position far mightier than any fallen angel. The Christians of the Bible went about preaching the gospel, not in frustration that territorial spirits were cramping their style, but in perfect confidence that God had already won the victory over them:

Rom 8:37-39 Nay, in all these things we are more than conquerors through him that loved us. For I am persuaded, that neither death, nor life, nor angels, nor principalities, nor powers, nor things present, nor things to come, Nor height, nor depth, nor any other creature, shall be able to separate us from the love of God, which is in Christ Jesus our Lord.

Eph 2:6 [God] hath raised us up together, and made us sit together in heavenly places in Christ Jesus: [who is]...

Eph 1:21-23 ...far above all principality, and power, and might, and dominion, and every name that is named, not only in this world, but also in that which is to come: And [The Father] hath put all things under his feet, and gave him to be the head over all things to the church.

But, I also would warn you to abstain from the new arrogance, the new confidence that "we understand in a deeper way than the early believers – we have new revelation; we have insight that they didn't have even in the early Church. We know more than the first disciples or the Church of a hundred years ago." This arrogance, of being the "cutting edge people" of a new age of global Christianity, is seducing many into adopting a dominionist agenda.

The Church Without Spot or Wrinkle?

Now, here is an oft-quoted scripture that is being misinterpreted in an alarming way. I don't believe it is an intentional misinterpreting, but oftentimes people will quote a portion of scripture as a buzzword. They say: "The Lord's coming back for a Church without spot or wrinkle."

Ephesians 5:25-27 Husbands, love your wives, even as Christ also loved the Church, and gave himself for it; that he might sanctify and cleanse it with the washing of water by the word, that he might present it to himself a glorious Church, not having spot, or wrinkle, or any such thing; but that it should be holy and without blemish.

What is implied in this interpretation is: "Hey, the Lord can't come back yet; we haven't got it together yet. We better clean up our act. Bring everybody together, we must get rid of spots or wrinkles."

I disagree entirely. That kind of thinking binds the Church and robs it of its blessed hope! Why? This is a man-centered view of life, like much of the Spiritual Warfare Movement. Ephesians

5:25-27 says, "Jesus will present to himself a glorious Church," not, "we better clean it up and come together, or Jesus can't come." Who is going to make the Church to be without spot or wrinkle? Us, or Jesus? The way you answer that question is crucial. Jesus will do it in us, at His coming. He's not waiting for us! We should be waiting for Him. No one can stop His coming again.

This kind of thinking is readily acceptable to people only when they look at the Church through carnal eyes. Many modern preachers focus on the spots and blemishes, saying, "How can Jesus come back when we are so divided?" Dear friend, the Church is not divided, because our unity is the unity of the Spirit. This hidden unity cannot be manufactured, only preserved. The Church was not started by the initiative of man, but by the initiative and action of the Lord Jesus Christ. It won't be perfected by man either, but by the Lord Jesus Christ, and it will also be glorified by the Lord Jesus Christ. "He will present to Himself a glorious Church, not having spot or wrinkle."

Pointing to the spots and blemishes that supposedly hold back the Lord from returning puts the onus and the guilt onto us. It rocks our confidence in God's ability to deal with His own Body. We stop seeing ourselves as more than conquerors, seated with Christ in the heavenlies, and start worrying about our spiritual condition on earth.

"If the Church Would Only Do Its Job"

A similarly destructive (yet so-called "humble") way of thinking starts out with statements like this: "If the Church was doing its job then...the world would be a better place, millions would flood into the kingdom, there'd be less crime and pornography, and so on." This puts the Church in bondage by making her responsible for the evils of the world. "If only we were doing our job..." Whatever happened to personal responsibility, or the judgment of God? What about the fact that this world rejects Christ because they choose to reject Christ? Did God tell us that "one day in the far distant future, the Church will get in gear; she will become militant, and then there will be a worldwide revival? Then, will whole nations – and even the world – will become "Christian?" No, God says, "Evil men shall wax worse and worse, deceiving and being deceived." "In the last days, perilous times shall come..." Notice, in predicting apostasy for the end times, God doesn't blame the Church for not doing her job.

Legalism comes in subtle ways, sometimes. The obvious legalism is righteousness by rules, standards, do's, and don'ts. The not-so-obvious legalism is the idea that everything operates by spiritual law. Therefore, if it's not happening, you aren't measuring up. You are not properly utilizing the spiritual laws? Right?

Here is a quote as an example. I'm quoting someone I believe to be a very sincere man with a valid, powerful ministry – John Dawson of YWAM.

> **In a global sense, each generation faces Satan in the form of the spirit of antichrist or world domination. This is the spirit behind those who have had ambition to rule the world such as Napoleon or Hitler. They would usurp the place that belongs only to God. The earth is the Lord's and all its fullness.(Psalm 24:1) A praying church should face this spirit and drive it off long before we find ourselves in a world at war.... The spirit of world domination can emerge only when the saints have lost their vigilance, or when the international Church has become severely divided over some issue.**[1]

I agree with many things Dawson says, but I take issue with this statement and its implications. Are we to hold the Church guilty for the world dominating spirit that provoked World War I and World War II? Is there going to be an Anti-Christ as a result of the Church letting her guard down? Aren't sinners really in rebellion against God? Have the churches of Los Angeles been held accountable by God for the recent riots there? If we stay vigilant can we prevent Revelation 13?

Actually, Jesus (for example) could not and would not stop the rich young ruler from walking away from His challenge to repent. There was rampant sin, legalism and pagan worship in the culture in which Jesus lived. Did God the Father accuse Jesus of failure because He didn't tackle those issues? Think about the Roman world of the first three centuries! Why didn't the church pray that "world dominating spirit" away?

Or, did God hold the early Church to blame for the intense persecution it endured at that time? No! Sin and sinners have their own agenda and their own impetus for rebelling against God's plan. The Church has rarely been in a position to influence world events in the sort of major way that John Dawson suggests.

Chapter Two Endnotes

1. Dawson, John. **Engaging the Enemy.** Introduction. Regal Books. Page x.

3

Man-Centered or God-Centered?

Here is a quote from Dick Bernal, from his book **Storming Hell's Brazen Gates**:

> I believe that on the day of Pentecost this is what happened. 120 prayer warriors – totally focused and in perfect harmony, blew open a hole so big that when the Spirit of God rushed through, the force of it sounded like a tornado.[1]

Sounds good doesn't it? This quote underscores the existence of two basic perspectives in the Pentecostal Evangelical world today. On the one hand, "We are so focused, we blew a hole through the heavens so we could usher in the Holy Spirit." On the other hand, God, the Sovereign Ruler of the universe, was pleased to pour out his Holy Spirit on weak, frightened, inadequate men, in spite of their unbelief, that He might be glorified. Think about it. Don't you see the contrast in this world today? Either, "We will ascend" or "He has descended."

Bernal's interpretation of Pentecost typifies the man-centered perspective that "We did it", through focus and unity. We achieved. Sure, we have to open a hole, so the Holy Ghost can get in, right?

Listen. Jesus isn't waiting for us to get it together. He can come back anytime He wants. Jesus is Lord. He doesn't need us, we need Him! When God is pleased to, He will be back. Yea, even when most people won't expect it. He is going to glorify the Church. It's not up to us. Maranatha, come quickly Lord Jesus! What He has started, He will finish, for all things are of Him and for Him!

The Dominion of Christ Over His Enemies

I challenge the way that I Corinthians 15:23, 27 and 28 is presently being interpreted:

But every man in his own order; Christ the firstfruits; afterward they that are Christ's at his coming. Then cometh the end, when He shall have delivered up the kingdom of God, even the Father; when He shall have put down all rule and all authority and power. For He must reign, till He hath put all enemies under His feet. The last enemy that shall be destroyed is death. For He hath put all things under his feet.

But when He saith all things are put under Him, it is manifest that He is excepted, which did put all things under Him. And when all things shall be subdued unto Him, then shall the Son also Himself be subject unto Him that put all things under Him, that God may be all in all.

Notice how many times the passage says, "He will" do something. It's not us, but Him! His initiative, His dominion, in His order and time, He will bring down all rebellion.

The new concept is that we will bring down dominions and powers. If only we could just get into unity, they say, if we could just learn to use the weapons of our warfare, and our authority. Then we would bring down all dominion, power, and authority. But, God says He (Jesus) is the one that is going to do it. This is part of the problem: there is a blurring of distinction between the identity of Jesus and the identity of the Church. We are not Christ. We are the Body of Christ, members of Christ, but we are not Christ Himself. It's "not I, but Christ." Christ is seated at the right hand of

God, but we are on earth, waiting for Christ, occupying, evangelizing, watching, and praying.

Note, verse 25 says, "He must reign until He has put all enemies under his feet." Verse 26, "The last enemy that shall be destroyed is death." I even know some people who believe we will destroy death! I know a man who says, "I'm not going to die!". His thinking is the end result of this idea. He doesn't believe he will die, but he also despises the Rapture! In other words, he wants to be glorified, but he doesn't want to allow Jesus to do it! It is God and not us, who puts Christ's enemies under His feet! See Psalm 110:1.

The Lord said unto my Lord, sit thou at my right hand, until I make thine enemies thy footstool.

An Old View of Victory

Victory, the old view, is through denial of self. Give up your life and you can have it! Jesus had to die a shameful death to attain the victory for all of us. Now, you hear teachers saying, "I'm tired of a sick, whipped, and defeated Church." Yet brokenness before God and renunciation of this life is our victory. Human pride and self-confidence are hindrances to victory.

A bad concept of victory leads to a wrong concept of the end times. I've heard this said many times: if nations aren't trembling at the feet of the Church; if they aren't coming to us to ask us, "how are you doing what your doing?"; if they are not awed by the wonderful, mighty works of the Church, then the Church is defeated, whipped, and failing its task.

But Jesus never told us the world would admire us, love us, respect us. Rather, the world will hate, despise, and reject you! The true Church has always been a despised minority.

Remember that there was a day when the nations trembled at the feet of the Church, but it wasn't in God's victory. It was the Papist, worldly, backslidden, politicized Church that controlled the world, as part of the Holy Roman Empire. The cross is victory, not self-confidence, or self-image. Those who die to self, and humble themselves are greatly used of God. He does not use the powerful, aggressive personalities, the confrontive preachers, the ones who are always after better performance, and so on. That is of the world. The ungodly, brash, militaristic air in the Church today is all too often mere worldliness, not spirituality.

Luke 18:8 *I tell you that he will avenge them speedily. Nevertheless when the Son of man cometh, shall he find faith on the earth?*

Jesus is questioning whether there will even be a biblical faith when He returns. If we are supposed to be so powerful, and successful – ruling, reigning, and tearing down strongholds – why is this question even necessary? We are being conditioned to believe in an all-powerful, much-admired, last days Church, instead of one that is following Him who was despised and rejected by the world, because of His truth! But Jesus had a different concept of the last days, "When I come back am I even going to find the original, biblical, faith on the face of the earth?" He will, but not to the universal degree that people are predicting.

Faith is presented today as a force or power with which to control circumstances – even to create a new society of godliness. But true faith has moral content, it makes demands of people. Faith takes the way of the cross, the way of denial. It involves the rejection of the flesh, the abandonment of self-confidence in the flesh. Faith is not an impersonal spiritual law. It is the abiding trust in Christ that causes people to give up on self and follow Him. Some teach we are in the God-class, having the faith of God. But we are not God! He is! We are not equal to God in any way, He created us and He alone is the object of our faith.

What is victory? I know a man who went so far with the idea of victory that he is now a Universalist. He is an elder in a Charismatic Church in Iowa, but he does not believe in an ultimate hell. I asked him, "Why don't you believe in an ultimate hell?" He said, "Are you trying to tell me in the end God will be defeated?" Is he saying that, if most people go to hell, God's going to be defeated? The truth is, if everyone went to hell, God has not been defeated. He won! He is forever vindicated. Why? He took on Himself the penalty of our sins, when He didn't have to! Through Christ He satisfied His own righteousness and His own mercy. He satisfied His righteousness by paying the death penalty that the law and holiness of God demands of the human race. He satisfied his mercy by making a way back to holiness, so whoever wants to, can be saved. No one can ever say God is not Holy, or God is not loving.

Don't judge God's success by human worldly standards, as some do by counting heads at the meeting, and boasting of how many came forward for prayer. Let God be justified even if everyone else is a liar! "That you might be justified when you speak, and vindicated when you are judged." (Romans 3:4)

If we judged Noah by worldly standards, we'd have to conclude he was a dismal failure. Why didn't God just teach Noah to bring down those ante-diluvian strongmen? How many were saved in the days of Noah? Eight. In those days, the population could easily have exceeded ours in number, and yet only eight were saved. Did God lose? Did Noah fail? No, the losers are those who adopt a worldly concept of victory.

Easy Believism

Luke 13:23-24 Then said one unto him, Lord, are there few that be saved? and he said unto them, Strive to enter in at the straight gate; for many, I say unto you, will seek to enter in, and shall not be able.

The Greek word for strive is: ἀγονιζομαι (agonizomai), agonize. The modern warfare doesn't have much agony and here is why. Focusing on demons and powers in the air allows me not to focus on repentance, brokenness, character, and humility. This is where I agree with John Dawson who teaches that much warfare is simply doing what the demons and selfish nature oppose. If pride is the issue, warfare is humbling yourself, submission, and so on. I agree! But, anybody, however carnal, can seem to "make war in the heavenlies". There's no struggle against the flesh involved. Devoted people, worldly people, all kinds of people are "tearing down principalities", but how many of them are tearing down the idols within their own hearts?

The biblical warning speaks thus: agonize, to enter in at the straight gate. The idea that it's easy to be saved is not true. It's not biblical. Agonize! You have to surrender self, and that can be the hardest thing of all. You have to deny self – and unfortunately we live in a culture that fosters self-love. Self can operate in defiance of God, without Satan.

This spiritual warfare movement alarms me because, in a subtle way, it promotes self. It says, "We are doing it...". We are bringing the Church together, we have spiritual revelation such as the apostles never had. And, if we are coming against "Ahab" or "Jezebel", or any other unscriptural notion, then we are special, we are really something.

Did the Apostles Practice It?

In fact, we are so special, we now "know" things poor old Paul the apostle didn't know. Paul didn't practice this brand of spiritual warfare, did he? None of the apostles "made war in the heavenlies", as we know it today. The apostles didn't bring down the principalities, powers, and dominions. At one point, after Jesus had sent the disciples out to preach, He said, "I saw Satan fall from heaven like lightning." The spiritual warfare people will say, "See, they pulled him down." But, no. The disciples did what scripture says they did – they preached the Gospel in every city, as the Lord commanded. They did cast out demons, a valid ministry.

Spiritual warfare is attacking the strongholds of people's ideas, in their minds. It is taking away the justifications, stripping away the excuses and reasonings, and the high things that exalt themselves against the knowledge of God. I'm talking about excuses such as, "I'm basically a good person." Someone needs to rise up and confront that kind of thinking with the law of God. Biblical spiritual warfare will challenge and demolish those imaginations with truth and in love. The law of God is an adequate weapon. If used rightly, it can convict the hardest heart, cutting down the proud in the imagination of their hearts.

We don't necessarily need to come against the spirit operating over a person, unless they are demonized, but, we do need to confront the person directly in their "vain imaginations". We need to reason with them like Paul did. Paul was stirred by the idols of Athens. But, he didn't try to pray Zeus or Mars or Hermes down from Athens. (Acts 17:22-31)

Chapter Three Endnotes

1. Bernal, Dick **Storming Hell's Brazen Gate**. Page 22.

4

A Warning To Charismatics

Matthew 7:21-23 Not everyone that saith unto me, Lord, Lord, shall enter into the kingdom of heaven; but he that doeth the will of my Father which is in heaven. Many will say to me in that day, Lord, Lord, have we not prophesied in thy name? and in thy name have cast out devils? and in thy name done many wonderful works? And then will I profess unto them, I never knew you; depart from me, ye that work iniquity.

  This is a frightening prospect to me. These are charismatic manifestations! We prophesied, we cast out devils, we did many wonderful works! And yet, Jesus says, "Depart from me ye workers of iniquity (lawlessness)." In other words, in spite of those scriptural things you did, you lived on your own terms – you did your own thing! I believe in casting out devils, speaking in tongues, healing, and good works. But, I believe many who do those things also do their own thing! "Wait a minute, Lord, we brought down that strongman. We fought war in the heavenlies. We were cutting edge." He will say, "You never submitted what you were doing to me for approval."
  The current idea of the Spiritual Warfare Movement is that we are going to be in charge. We will be taking over cities and nations for Jesus. On the other hand, Jesus wondered if the Son of Man would even find faith on the earth when He returned. The biblical gospel will never be popular, because the cross doesn't exalt man, it humbles him. It doesn't put man in control, it puts God on the

throne. This is never going to change. God's message has never been palatable to natural man and it never will be. The world can never participate in the gospel message because what we believe is an offence to them, a scandal. Denial of self? Are you kidding?

Other Misconceptions

Here are a couple of quotes to show the kind of thing I'm talking about. These are from the book, **Engaging the Enemy**. It is an anthology of some of the best from the Warfare Movement.

> **Orlando, Florida. Cars barely crawl along South Orange Blossom Trail on this Friday night. Commuters head home, tourists wind their way to the hotel, men try to go unnoticed as they enter the topless bars that line the street. Jim Gaines, a balding 50 year old elder, pulls his car into the parking space across the street from the adult bookstore. He shuts off the headlights and turns off the engine and quotes II Corinthians 10:4, "For the weapons of our warfare are not carnal, but mighty through God to the pulling down of strongholds". For the next 30 minutes he and two other people in the car praise God and rebuke the devil as they and several others have for several months.**

Well, first of all, I believe in prayer. Praise God for people like Jim Gaines. If there was a true spirit of prayer in Pentecostal circles, we probably wouldn't be dealing with much of this error. Read on:

> **We bind the spirits of lust and sexual perversion in this place. We marshal angels to take charge and speak to the hearts of the men who enter this building.**

Jesus said He has given his angels charge concerning us. But, the modern concept is that we tell the angels what to do and where to go. There is man's arrogance again.

> **Two weeks later and a half a mile down the road at a combined meeting of several Orlando churches, Metro Life Church pastor Danny Jones leads about 500 Christians in prayer for the city. Then they enter into spiritual warfare, denouncing the demonic spirits that**

blind the eye of Christians in the city, and pulling down the strongholds that rule over the region. Specifically they denounce the spirits that control the adult entertainment businesses that sell pornography. Within a month the city's Metropolitan Board of Investigation has enough evidence to start legal proceedings that could close the adult bookstores.[1]

I'm glad that's happening. I'm glad people are praying together. I hate pornography. But, what if overnight you could eradicate all porn in Orlando, Florida? Would Orlando be all right then? Would the people in Orlando be less lustful in their hearts? I am truly grateful for any suppression of blatant sin, but let's not mistake that for salvation, or even victory.

Choose Your Battles – Are we Fighting the Right Enemy?

In our own city, Christians are mobilizing to campaign for better television. Is it good to sit and watch secular TV at all? Did God call us to clean up TV? There is a new show that aired this Fall called "NYPD Blue." Christians marched, prayed, commanded, and rebuked to get it off the air (the show is trash, absolutely). What if we win that battle – is TV ok now?

Part of the confusion for spiritual people nowadays is not knowing what battles to fight. What are we standing for? Better TV? I hope not. There is a misplaced emphasis. Even if we prevailed and there was perfectly wholesome TV, what have we really accomplished? TV is no substitute for prayer, communication, and family care.

As well as that, have you ever considered we could be fighting God? God may be showing us the true nature of TV by allowing the filth to be exposed.

Nahum 3:5-6 Behold, I am against thee, saith the Lord of hosts; and I will discover thy skirts upon thy face, and I will shew the nations thy nakedness, and the kingdoms thy shame. And I will cast abominable filth upon thee, and make thee vile, and will set thee as a gazingstock.

God may well be allowing nudity to be on TV so that His people will turn if off once and for all, and realize that only prayer and communication satisfies your spirit. There is no substitute for seeking God. No substitute for Koinonia (fellowship).

The Bible says that in the last days the devil will wear out the saints. Think of all the money, time, effort, energy, and air time to "get NYPD Blue (and similar stuff) off the air". On TV, bad is a relative term. For instance, fifteen years ago, the show "Roseanne" wouldn't have been allowed on the air. It has no nudity, yet. But, so what? Already, on that show, God is mocked, the family bashed, authority is derided, lesbianism is promoted – but at least there is no nudity! So the reasoning goes. Heaven help us! To be consistent, we should be combatting Barney and Sesame Street, they promote ungodly values as well.

No wonder people are confused. We can only fight the enemies of faith as God permits and as God discloses them to us. To initiate projects of warfare outside God's will only leads to confusion or defeat and – on top of which – the Lords' Name is brought into disrepute when aggressive agitators, acting in His name, aim their offensives at the wrong targets.

Attacking Your City

Pastor Dick Bernal of San Jose, California, and his church, Christian Jubilee Christian Center, joined with other churches to "attack" their city. This church believed in intercessory prayer with a twist. They rented rooms on the top floors of hotels, or assembled on the tops of hills, or the rooftops of tall buildings. (Doesn't the Bible say something about high places?)

You see, through researching his city's history back to the California Gold Rush, Bernal says that the type of people attracted by instant riches produced the "Spirit of Greed."

Well, I beg to differ. The problem is not localized to a "Spirit of Greed". The problem is the fallen human condition. But it's easier to deal with the spirit of this or the spirit of that than to confront people with the depravity of fallen, rebellious man. There is no particular type of person attracted to instant riches. All people are the same the world over. Men are fallen, depraved, sinful, greedy, putting themselves first. Tell them that this sort of behaviour is caused by a "spirit of greed" and they happily amen you, relieved of their own moral accountability.

Allow me to quote Bernal:
> **We were concerned that the San Francisco/San Jose/Oakland area sits alone as the only major metropolis in the US never to experience a major revival. Quickly the principality of "Self" was identified as dominant.**[2]

Oh, now I get it! Self is a spirit, a principality! Cast self out and you have no more greed? Rent the 13th floor of a hotel, pray against "'Self', out there", bring it down from the heavenlies. What deception! This is actually self-exalting, not self-denying! "We brought down 'Self' last night! Praise God!" No, this is deception. 'Self' is not out there, it is in us and you can't cast **him** out!

I really don't like to write on this level. Like Jude, I would love to just talk about salvation. But, there are certain men who have crept in unawares. They are appealing to a love of self in people, which seduces them away from the message of the cross. All false teachers do is appeal to what we already want. We don't like repentance. It's more fun to go out and "attack" an external enemy than to confront the iniquity within. Going out with "warfare prayer and warfare worship" makes people feel like they are accomplishing something. It's much more gratifying than prayer, repentance, and waiting on God.

We would rather come against Jezebel and Ahab out there, than take time to love our wives and children, pay our bills, and live right. "Christians gathered around the high places of San Jose to start with praise and worship." Jesus said it doesn't matter where you worship (high places?!). However, what is the focus of this sort of warfare praise? Is it in praise of the sheer glory of God or is it "aiming" praise to unseat the enemy?

Remember, "Only the Strong Survive", "We can do it", "Making War in the Heavenlies". Can you see where the emphasis has changed? What is the content of the worship songs? God, the cross, heaven? Or war, Satan, our victory, us?

Two Principles at Work

I can truly sum it up like this. There are two principles at work in the world today – the mystery of iniquity (lawlessness), and the mystery of godliness.

What is the mystery of iniquity? It can be summed up like this: We (men) will exalt ourselves to the level of God. Satan, Adam and Eve, the builders of Babel, all of these, tried to exalt themselves. They promoted themselves to ascend to God's level. They said, we are the cutting edge, we can bring down the principalities, and so forth.

The mystery of godliness is the opposite principle. God descends to us, as in the incarnation. Man is too depraved to ascend, God must descend. Which side is more popular? The mystery of iniquity, by far! If I can bring down the prince of self, (external), instead of repent, (internal), I'd rather do the first, any day. This is the principle underlying every false spiritual philosophy today: "We can ascend." But it can only be one or the other. Either we can do it, as in "Only the strong survive", or, "No, I have to wait for God to save me, to rescue me, to break through on my behalf." This way of thinking, the two principles, separates the human race into two religions. It is either Cain or Abel. Man ascending to God's level on his own terms or God coming down to save us.

What could be a greater contrast between Adam and Christ? Adam, like others, was not content with being a mere man, a lowly believer and worshipper. He came to believe, (new revelation!), that there was a spiritual experience, a knowledge that could exalt him to godhood.

On the other hand, Jesus, who actually is God, did not regard equality with God something to grasp, but emptied Himself and became a servant, and actually obeyed the Father to His own death! It is His attitude that we are to have and hold!

Chapter Four Endnotes

1. Wagner, C. Peter. **Engaging the Enemy**. Jubilee Christian Center. Pages 22-23.
2. Ibid, page 36.

5

Presumptuous Are They!

Oh, if I could just write about God's love, salvation, grace, or faith! But certain ones have crept in unawares, and they have become widely accepted, seducing the Church.

2 Peter 2:9-11 *The Lord knoweth how to deliver the godly out of temptations, and to reserve the unjust unto the day of judgment to be punished: But chiefly them that walk after the flesh in the lust of uncleanness, and despise government. Presumptuous are they, self-willed, they are not afraid to speak evil of dignities. Whereas angels, which are greater in power and might, bring not railing accusation against them before the Lord.*

Jude 9-10 *Yet Michael the archangel, when contending with the devil he disputed about the body of Moses, durst not bring against him a railing accusation, but said, The Lord rebuke thee. But these speak evil of those things which they know not; but what they know naturally, as brute beasts, in those things they corrupt themselves.*

Many, who promote spiritual warfare, love God with all their heart. They want revival, but they are resorting to the flesh. Revival is not initiated by man, but by God. God is sovereign in revival. We can't presume on revival. There may be another revival, if it pleases God, but we can't presumptuously assume that. We must ask God for the showers. We can't make it happen by our own efforts.

Spiritual warfare teachers would have you believe that the disciples in the upper room "opened the way for" the Holy Ghost. But they weren't blasting a hole through the heavenlies! They were weak and scared. They had locked themselves away in that upper room.

But, presumption is so abundant in the Church now! Look at the Christian media! Self-will! Arrogant pride! In these verses above, "dignities" are fallen angelic entities. Just because Satan fell from grace does not mean he lost his substance. Look at Jude 9 again! God still calls Satan the prince of this world. They are still called principalities, powers, thrones, and rulers of the darkness of this age. They still have places of authority. Their time is coming, their doom is sure, but not by our hand. The Lord Himself will destroy them with the brightness of his coming and the Spirit of His mouth! (2 Thess 2:8) We may overcome them now in our personal walk, but we can't banish them!

People are fighting against Jezebel, Ahab, and a host of other named strongmen, (names that the Bible does not reveal as belonging to principalities). But why didn't the apostles know about this? Better yet, why didn't Jesus know? When Paul went to Corinth, did he research the history of the city to find out the "strongman"? A quick check would have revealed spirits of lust. The book of Acts and the letters Paul wrote to the Corinthians are strangely silent about such a strategy. What about Ephesus and its spirits of witchcraft? Did Paul exhort the Ephesians to come against Diana? Beware of any practice unknown to the apostles.

According to spiritual warfare theory, Jesus should have researched the city of Jerusalem. He wept over Israel that they did not recognize the time of their visitation. Why didn't He come directly against spirits of religion and legalism through warfare prayer? When Jesus revealed to John, in the book of Revelation, about the city of Pergamos, He told him exactly where Satan's seat is. But, did He say, "John, you can strike a real blow for the Church. Come against Satan. Have a city-wide meeting at Pergamos. Bring him down!" No. He said, "Satan is going to cast you into prison for ten days." Does that sound victorious to you?

We have to understand victory by God's standard. Jesus told them to be faithful, even in tribulation. Can you see the difference between the two philosophies? When some people moan, "I'm tired of a whipped Church, tired of a broken Church, a divided Church," I think they are tired of the reproach of the cross.

Every time the Church has the "upper hand" over the world, evil comes of it. Think of the days of the Roman Popes or Calvin's Geneva. They had all the political power and popularity they could have wanted, but power corrupts.

2 Peter 2:11 *Whereas angels, which are greater in power and might, bring not railing accusation against them before the Lord.*

It is dangerous and unhealthy to study about the names of some of these spirits and their characteristics, and to name them Jezebel spirit, Ahab spirit, and so on. The Bible doesn't teach it, and the apostles didn't practise it. Even the angels of God, who actually know these spirits accurately, will dare not take this presumptuous, confident, even aggressive attitude. (See Jude 9)

Railing accusations? These people have these spirits named, described, and lately even mapped! There is a brash, cocky attitude.

Railing Accusations

Jude 8 *Likewise also these filthy dreamers defile the flesh, despise dominion, and speak evil of dignities.*

This is a quote from **Engaging the Enemy**:

> More than any place I know the most prominent Christian leaders in Argentina, such as Omar Cabreo and Carlos Annacondia, Hector Gimenez, and others, overtly challenge and curse Satan and his demonic forces both in private prayer and in public platforms. The nation as a whole is apparently engaged in a world class power encounter.[1]

To challenge and curse Satan publicly sounds like a violation of Jude 9 if I ever heard one! It even gets more bizarre: Paul Lehmann, a missionary to Zaire with Christian and Missionary Alliance, recently published a list of nine names of demons he cast out of a witch doctor, Tata Pembele.[2] At the end of the list the book says, "Through them the witch doctor had exercised greater power."

Now, how do you get these names of demons? Interview the demon-possessed? I can see it now, "You lying spirit, tell me the truth!" I did not reprint the names of the spirits in the paragraph above because of a specific scripture:

Joshua 23: 7-8 That ye come not among these nations, these that remain among you; neither make mention of the name of their gods, nor cause to swear by them, neither serve them, nor bow yourselves unto them: But cleave unto the Lord your God, as ye have done unto this day.

I believe there is a deep defilement for anyone who becomes morbidly fascinated with demons and their names. "Neither make mention of their names." Remember, we know only what God has revealed. He only reveals what is needful for us. Beware the abundance of extra-biblical revelation. The knowledge of the so-called deep things of Satan will not give you victory in spiritual warfare:

Revelation 2:24-25 But unto you I say, and unto the rest in Thyatira, as many as have not this doctrine, and which have not known the depths of Satan, as they speak; I will put upon you none other burden. But that which ye have already hold fast till I come.

We overcome him, by the blood of the Lamb, reconciliation to God, the word of our testimony, (do we agree with the message of the blood?), and because we love not our life to death, (no self justification, but justifying God only).

Allow me to give you Dick Bernal's extra biblical "revelation" of how to wage warfare for a city. To take our cities we should:

1. **Proclaim a fast with prayer;**
2. **Identify the principality over the city;**
3. **Determine its geographical location;**

4. Call him/her by name. We know our chief adversary by name and title; some are Satan, belial, devil, prince, dragon, serpent, adversary, accuser, wicked one, enemy, tempter, and thief.[3]

Well, number one is fasting and prayer. Amen. I agree wholeheartedly, hallelujah! Many of the spiritual warfare leaders have a deep desire for the Church to return to a devoted spirituality and I applaud it. Definitely, Christians should return to fasting and prayer.

Number two, identify the principality. Well, as I observed earlier, Paul didn't know about this step in Corinth, or Ephesus. Why didn't he tell the Romans to do this, in his letter to them? For that matter, Jesus could have used this step on Tyre, Sidon, or Jerusalem. Beware of the unapostolic revelation! But this step is given so matter-of-factly and authoritatively, it disarms some. Let this writing be a call for discernment, Lord.

Number three is truly puzzling. How do you determine the actual geographic location of a principality? According to Bernal, fasting and prayer should reveal the physical location of the principality:

> **Even the ancient Greeks knew how to approach their gods (whom we now identify as principalities). They were always approached by name and title. I am presently convinced that through prayer and fasting, the Spirit of God will show us who and where these present rulers are. Only then will we be able to focus our militant prayers like a rifle, (as opposed to our present buckshot approach), taking keen aim at our adversary and allowing God to work through us to bring down these gates of brass.**[4]

Now the ancient Greeks and their gods are the standard by which we measure spiritual warfare? This is what happens when Christians attempt to operate without objective revelation. Peter says that because of the sensuality of some, the way of truth will be evil spoken of. Sensuality does not always equate to sexuality. It means that you approach spirituality through the senses, trying to reduce the spiritual realm into physical dimensions. I can't trust pagan insight into how to approach demons.

Dick Bernal is saying here that there is an address, a place in the city where the principality is located. This is a harmful way of thinking. It encourages carnal Christians to look for and locate demons, principalities, or dignitaries, that even the angels dare not revile. Although this information is misleading it truly does involve very real and very dangerous entities.

Also, we develop a misplaced emphasis. What if all this energy went into evangelism? Furthermore, this is dangerous because principalities are real! They are nothing to trifle with. We are not to go beyond "what is written", especially in our dealing with the adversary. When we have to study the demon-possessed witch doctor, occultists, or the culture of the pagan ancient Greeks for "insight" we know we are off base!

Alas, so many are soulish and sensual, today. They find it so much better to locate the strongman of a city than to confront the sinner in his way with the claims of Christ. God help us, in these last days! We have to remember that operating outside of biblical revelation opens us up to powerful deception. Anyone can be deceived, even the sincere. We aren't the "special generation", a "new breed of overcomers". We are redeemed human beings, frail vessels, washed in the blood of Jesus. Sorry, but that's the way it is!

Back to the fourth step: call him/her by name in prayer. Where in scripture do you ever see anything even close to this list? Do we know more now than Paul and Peter? Name one place on the globe that has no demonic influence. There is no vacuum in the spirit world. When the prince of Persia is expelled, the prince of Greece comes in. Stay in your own God-given sphere, and leave it alone! God has for some reason ordained these "princes" and their sphere of influence. Breakthroughs have more to do with prayer and heartfelt repentance than "warfare"! (See 2 Chronicles 7:14). When the time comes He, not us, will bring down all thrones, rulers, dominions, and powers. He set them up and He will put them down.

Psalm 62:11 *God hath spoken once; twice have I heard this; that power belongeth unto God.*

Psalm 75:1-8 *Unto thee, O God, do we give thanks, unto thee do we give thanks; for that thy name is near thy wondrous works declare. When I shall receive the congregation I will judge uprightly. The earth and all the inhabitants thereof are dissolved: I bear up the pillars of it. Selah. I said unto the fools, Deal not foolishly; and to the wicked, Lift not up the horn: Lift not up your horn on high: speak not with a stiff neck. For promotion cometh neither from the east, nor from the west, nor from the south. But God is the judge: he putteth down one, and setteth up another. For in the hand of the Lord there is a cup, and the wine is red; it is full of mixture; and he poureth out of the same: but the dregs thereof, all the wicked of the earth shall wring them out, and drink them.*

The Church as Scapegoat

The problem is we have become man-centered. It is all up to us. When are we going to rise up? According to the faulty concept of evangelism, here is why people aren't being saved:

• Number One: The Church is so divided, that people can't be saved. That's why we have to get rid of doctrine (truth) and build a unity based on love. Only then will people turn to Jesus.

• Number Two: People also can't be saved, supposedly, because we need to break the power of the devil over their life. If the devil isn't being broken who is at fault? You've got it, us!

• Number Three: The church doesn't have enough power, signs or wonders. According to Rodney Howard-Browne, an evangelist who calls himself, "God's Bartender,"[5]

> **The youngsters are turning to rock music, drugs, alcohol and free sex, and the yuppie generation is turning to the New Age Movement. There are two reasons for this. One, they have a hunger in their hearts for something that is real. Two, the church is not meeting or fulfilling their need and instead has become a referral system.**[6]

There you have it, they really want something real, but the church won't give it, because she doesn't have it!

- Number Four: We are told repeatedly, people aren't being saved because of ignorance. They have never seen genuine Christianity, certainly not in the Church. Guess what, we again are at fault.

When this is promoted often enough, God's people accept it. But think about it this way, was Noah held responsible for the low conversion rate of his day? (8 souls).

What about the biggest reason of all that people are not being saved, that is, they don't want to! They reject bowing the knee to the Lord Jesus Christ. They don't want to get right with God. It's not that the Church is failing to do its job, but that people are rebels, remember? They are wilfully ignorant of God and they will be held accountable.

Romans 1:18 *For the wrath of God is revealed from heaven against all ungodliness and unrighteousness of men, who hold the truth in unrighteousness;* [Hold = suppress]

People are not ignorant of God, they just hate Him. They suppress His truth in their minds so they won't have to think about Him. They love it when Christians blame their rejection of Him on other Christians. Sinners always love to justify themselves. If Christians want to change anything, they should change their unbiblical view of sinners and go back to Romans chapter one, two, and three. Then we will began to preach a gospel that has teeth – conviction of sin and the law of God. The true gospel will stop every mouth and convict the whole world as guilty before God. Only after establishing the guiltiness of mankind can we preach love, grace, and forgiveness.

Rejection of the Rapture

The Rapture is another doctrine under fire. There is a scoffing and mocking of the "escape theory". Why? The Rapture is another doctrine that reinforces our inability to save ourselves, nor our world. We must be "delivered from the evils of this present world" by a God who descends to snatch us up. No, we can't ascend higher and higher, taking over the kingdoms of this world. Don't flatter yourself. The Rapture sets people's eyes on heaven, and that's why it is scoffed at by earthly-minded people.

The Bible tells us, *Our citizenship is in heaven, from which we await the Saviour, the Lord Jesus Christ, who will change our vile bodies.* This is the hope of Christians, one which glorifies God, not man. But many Christians are being duped into an emphasis on dominion and control of this world.

Listen to a quote from Gary North:

Heaven is for dead men in Christ, the earth is for living men in Christ.[7]

Doesn't that just make you want to go there? Not if you are bombarded with that stuff!

I don't want to stay on this earth. I am a pilgrim. I am not trying to reform this earth, though I do hope to make an impact for Christ while I am here. This world is under the judgment of God. Even if we do clean up television and it gets semi-bad, instead of abominable like it is today, then all we have done is to draw a nice picture in the sand, only to see it washed away by the next wave. God hasn't called us to reform this world system, not even abortion reform. Certainly I've stood out in front of abortion clinics and preached, but not for the political impact, not to lobby people, or convey favour or support. I've preached out there because that is where more souls need to be confronted with the Word of God's judgment and His mercy in Christ! But, I really want to go to heaven and be with my Saviour.

Our life on this earth is short. If Satan can keep us busy doing "good", changing earthly legislation, fighting "strongmen", or anything to keep us from our actual calling – the simplicity of preaching The Gospel – then he will. But, preaching Christ and praying doesn't seem adequate to many, in order to meet modern challenges. This is why evangelism could decrease as spiritual warfare and political activism increase. As Christian energy and zeal is misplaced, and as other churches unite with evangelicals for "warfare" and activism, evangelism will definitely decrease. After all, who are you to witness to that Catholic or Mormon, who protests that clinic with you, or that Lutheran who participates in "March for Jesus" with you?

As a matter of fact, several months after this previous point was written, the Evangelical/Catholic Accord was announced. The document is called "Evangelicals and Catholics Together: The Christian Mission in the Third Millennium." Here is an excerpt from their news release.

> They toiled together in the movements against abortion and pornography and now leading Catholics and Evangelicals are asking their flocks for a remarkable leap of faith, to finally accept each other as Christians.

Some of the Evangelical leaders who signed the accord, which amounts to an agreement to stop proselytization, were Pat Robertson, Charles Colson, Bill Bright, Os Guinness, J. I. Packer, and Herbert Schlossberg. Note, one of the primary concerns was the political coalition that was formed – that perhaps too much preaching and sound doctrine might jeopardize. Remember, if Christianity includes everybody, then it means nothing.

False Confirmation

Allow me to share another quote from **Engaging the Enemy**:

> The dominating characteristic of spirits over cities can be greed, in New York; power, in Washington, DC; pornography in LA; lust, timidity, pride, or other sin.[8]

Fine, you've got the spirits identified! (Are you sure those aren't sinful characteristics of men, worldwide?) If you "know" what these "spirits" are, what progress have you made over them? Has "greed" been broken in New York? If it has, are the people now better off? I know of a minister who went to a conference in a major city in Alabama and he excitedly told me of a "sign" that the conference was impacting the city. The city had a huge statue of Vulcan, the Greek god of fire, set in a prominent place. During the conference the statue began to crack and pieces fell off to the point where the city had to cordon off the statue. Beware of sensual confirmations. Is that city now better off? What are the signs of the kingdom of God – crumbling statues or changed hearts?

Romans 14:17 *For the kingdom of God is not meat and drink; but righteousness, and peace, and joy in the Holy Ghost.*

It is not my intention to be critical, but we have to take seriously the prospect of a worldwide deception based on "lying signs and wonders". If it were possible even the elect might be deceived! Vulcan crumbling is along the same lines as the statue of the Virgin weeping, hardly a God-given confirmation!

The Real Problem

At the risk of sounding repetitious, Satan is strategizing against us, attempting to misplace our focus. There is a misplaced emphasis on the demonic. Scripture tells us that there is coming a thousand year period of universal rest and peace. Satan will be bound, righteousness will reign from the throne of David, the throne of the Lord Jesus Christ. Yet, at the end of that blissful, long awaited period, men will rebel against God. Satan will be loosed and will find ample recruits for a massive, though short lived, uprising. What is my point? We don't have near as big a problem from Satan as we do from self!

Ironically there is much scorning of a literal Millennium among these warfare teachers! Why? The Millennium proves our point. One thousand years of perfect environment, no devil or principalities, the Church being everything it is supposed to be, and yes, at the end, another worldwide rebellion!

So, the problem isn't really the presence of Satan and his angels. I wish it were that simple. We could just "use our authority" and cast him out and come into a new day of gospel dominion. Right? Then when we have subdued all rule and dominion, gotten our act together, and become all we can be as the Church, then Christ can come back and we can hand the world over to him. Is that how it should be?

1 Corinthians 15:23-27 But every man in his own order: Christ the firstfruits; afterward they that are Christ's at his coming. Then cometh the end, when he shall have delivered up the kingdom to God, even the Father, when he shall have put down all rule and all authority and power. For he must reign, till he hath put all enemies under his feet. The last enemy that shall be destroyed is death. For he hath put all things under his feet. But when he saith, all things are put under him, it is manifest that he is expected, which did put all things under him, that God may be all in all.

No, the real problem is pride. Man at the center, even redeemed man, constantly wanting to assert self. There is a lack of brokenness, little compassion for souls, a man-centered gospel, and a desperate need to seek God. It seems we Americans are always looking for the new and improved way!

Paul knew something about spiritual warfare:

Acts 16: 16-20 And it came to pass, as we went to prayer, a certain damsel possessed with a spirit of divination met us, which brought her masters much gain by soothsaying: The same followed Paul and us, and cried, saying, These men are the servants of the most high God, which shew unto us the way of salvation. And this did she many days. But Paul, being grieved, turned and said to the spirit, I command thee in the name of Jesus Christ to come out of her. And he came out the same hour. And when her masters saw that the hope of their gains was gone, they caught Paul and Silas, and drew them into the marketplace unto the rulers, and brought them to the magistrates, saying, these men being Jews, do exceedingly trouble our city.

At Philippi Paul confronted literally a Pythian spirit in this girl. He cast the spirit out of her, but this didn't "loose" the Philippians to receive salvation. On the contrary, they were angry and beat Paul and Silas and cast them into jail.

Did Paul and Silas go down into their cell saying, "We come against this Pythian spirit, this Roman spirit, you come down strongman over Philippi!?" No, they sang praises to God! The biblical emphasis, the focus, is on God! It was as they sang praises unto God that everything started shaking!

Paul didn't come against Hermes in Athens, Zeus in Corinth, or Romulus in Rome. He didn't need to research the history of Ephesus. He was a God-centered man! No statues crumbled in Athens as a confirmation of Paul's message. A few hard hearts did, though.

Another spiritual warfare teacher told me, "We had a conference in Washington DC and Deception was revealed as the strongman." (What discernment!) "We came against deception in prayer and the next days headlines read, 'Deception Exposed In The City Government'." I would say to that: two or three years later is there any less deception in Washington, DC?

I believe that earnest people have been in violation of scripture for so long, without being challenged, that lying signs and wonders are now seeming to "confirm" these things. We should no longer be asking, "Is this being confirmed by a sign?" Rather, "What is the nature of the sign?"

Is God really using crumbling statues or newspaper headlines? What are the marks of a true confirmation? That it glorifies Jesus. That it actually benefits people as being from God. Also, are these confirming signs scriptural? People need to be retrained to look at things this way, and to make a critical analysis in the light of scripture.

Five Criteria By Which To Judge

I will close this section of the book with some crucial premises by which to judge any new movement that comes to the Church.

1. Is it man-exalting?

Any teaching that exalts men is popular now. If you title a book, "The Application of the Cross", "Steps to Self-Improvement", or "Improving Your Self Image", which one will sell more books? I have been demonstrating to you that the Spiritual Warfare Movement is man-exalting. We are making war in the heavenlies.

We are taking whole cities for Christ. We are the victorious Church!

   2. Is it true to the established Word of God?

Do Dick Bernal, John Dawson, and others I have quoted now have new truth? I am sure they would say, this isn't new truth, it is old truth that the Church has neglected and is being restored. Well, did the apostles have this truth? I think not. If it wasn't for the apostles, it is not for the Church today. "To the law and the testimony. If they speak not according to this word, there is no light in them." We are not a special generation with new revelation!

   3. Is it based on human perceptions of "success"?

But Pastor Bill, they do this warfare in Central and South America and it works! This is the fatal, flawed type of thinking to which many appeal, and to which thousands subscribe. It works, pragmatism, if it works it must be right. Well, then Noah wasn't right. He only had eight converts. No earth shaking revival! Or, Samson was right in every area of his life because he had great results against the Philistines! We flatter ourselves. Yes, there are great revivals going on in South and Central America. But why? We are duped into thinking, "These spiritual warfare techniques must be working." Right? But what about God? Don't you think a revival is an example of God working mightily to save, in spite of men? I believe that there is revival going on in Argentina because God is sovereignly pleading for that country and the hour of their visitation had come, not, as **Engaging the Enemy** reports, because "Omar Cabrera, Carlos Annacondia and Hector Gimenez are overtly challenging and cursing Satan and his demonic forces."[9]

   4. Does it teach that man rises to "the God level," or that God descends to man?

The lie and the truth are two specific principles. Mysteries are what scripture calls them. The mystery of lawlessness is one principle that undergirds most of society, even religion. It teaches us that we can ascend, and be like the Most High (who puts down thrones and exalts). It teaches that we, men and women, can control. We can dominate! The truth is, God has to descend, to save us. This is the reason that the world despises the incarnation, as well as the Rapture, and the Millennium.

John 3:13 *And no man ascended up to heaven, but he that came down from heaven, even the Son of man which is in heaven.*

You see, God has to intervene, to condescend and save us by His grace, He enters our condition. We are too weak, bankrupt, and empty to save ourselves. We need God. He doesn't truly need us. One mystery (the lie) exalts us while the other (the truth) humbles us.

Receiving the Love of the Truth

God is not removing the false prophets and teachers. He is actually using them to test our hearts. Some of us need to be tested in the area of control, others pride, others self-sufficiency.

2 Thessalonians 2:9-12 *Even him, whose coming is after the working of Satan with all power and signs and lying wonders, and with all deceivableness of unrighteousness in them that perish; because they received not the love of the truth, that they might be saved. And for this cause God shall send them strong delusion, that they should believe a lie: That they all might be damned who believed not the truth, but had pleasure in unrighteousness.*

In these last days we are warned that people will be deceived because of one particular sin: they would not receive the love of the truth. You think you have received the truth, just because it works? Something that "works" for you is not necessarily true according to scripture, which is the only real plumbline. We need to drop our pragmatism and follow truth for truth's sake!

I don't follow Christ because it improves my marriage, or self-image, or whatever. I follow Him because He is truth, regardless of "results", no matter what it costs.

5. Does it deflect honest criticism?

Finally, there is the whole subject of criticism. There is a strange idea in the Church today that says "judge not, all criticism is bad!" I see Satan behind that, trying to side track the critical thinking called discernment, that we need so desperately in these days. No one can be criticized anymore, it's divisive! No one, that is, but those who dare question anyone else.

Yet it is possible to make a critical judgment without being unloving or unfair. Matthew 7 teaches us never to criticize mercilessly. It tells us to be subject to the same standards by which we judge others – true judgment is scrupulously fair and impartial, as well as merciful and generous. I have quoted some people and mentioned some names here, but not to harm or destroy. I certainly wouldn't question the devotion and dedication and fruitfulness of these ministries. However, if the Pentecostal Movement is to be safeguarded against the deception about which Jesus and the apostles prophesied, we have to allow for open discussion and disagreement. I welcome this kind of dialogue about anything I have ever spoken or written.

However, Satan would silence those who have been called "Heresy Hunters". He always wants to silence honest criticism so as to be free to act in perfect liberty, without any examination of his words and deeds. Many teachers have taken on this same defensive spirit. Are we to become as the world, that now refuses to make any distinction between right and wrong? Or are we to obey the command of scripture, to "judge righteous judgment"?

Even as the world is becoming indiscriminate, rejecting belief in absolute truth, so the Church has become indiscriminate also. You can believe almost anything and be accepted by the Christian media now. The only sin even recognized now is "judging" – that is, saying that any teaching, or practice is unscriptural. That is now considered to be divisive. This sort of failure to make a distinction makes us tremendously vulnerable to the enemy. After all, many have forsaken their doctrine (truth) in the name of unity! Ironically, with all the talk about spiritual warfare, this is an aspect of spiritual warfare (contending for the faith) that is vitally important, but in their blindness and arrogance, too many are unable to see! Well, let's open our eyes and admit "the emperor has no clothes!"

There is some bitter medicine we have to swallow. These practices are not scriptural, and this unity without a doctrinal foundation is highly dangerous. Let's be bold enough to say that the average high churchman is not saved, and that we need to witness to him, not just accept him as a brother in unity. We desperately need to hold fast to good doctrine no matter how it divides. There, that wasn't so bad now, was it?

Chapter Five Endnotes

1. Wagner, C. Peter. **Engaging the Enemy**. Page 46.
2. Ibid. Page 48.
3. Bernal, Dick. **Storming Hell's Brazen Gate**. Page 55.
4. Ibid. Page 57.
5. Duin, Julia. **Charisma**. August, 1994. Page 21.
6. Browne, Rodney Howard. **The Touch of God**. RHBEA Publications. Page 4.
7. Balyeat, Joseph, **The Great Whore of Babylon Revealed**. From Introduction.
8. Lawson, Steve. **Engaging the Enemy**. Chapter Two "Defeating Territorial Spirits." Page 32.
9. Wagner, C. Peter. **Engaging the Enemy**. Page 46.

Part Two

6

What Is True Spiritual Warfare?

The Scriptural Use of Spiritual Warfare

I now would like to shift this discussion from criticism of current beliefs to affirmation of the orthodox beliefs about spiritual warfare. There is much good material out there on this subject. Certainly, we are in a war. Right from the beginning the Bible established this truth.

***Genesis 3:15** And I will put enmity between thee and the woman, and between thy seed and her seed; it shall bruise thy head, and thou shalt bruise his heel.*

In this verse we see that the seed of the serpent would oppose the seed of the woman. The outcome is never in doubt: "It shall crush thy head" – but there will be a cost, "Thou (the serpent) shalt bruise his heel." This can be understood on at least two levels of interpretation. On Calvary, the seed of the woman, virgin-born

Jesus, crushed the head of the serpent, but victory was accomplished by the bruising of our Lord's heel.

But equally, the seed of the woman can refer to the "seed" of Christ, the believers, and the seed of the serpent can certainly refer to the demonic realm, or the wicked:

Matthew 13:38 The field is the world; the good seed are the children of the kingdom; but the tares are the children of the wicked one.

Until Christ returns, spiritual tension is assured. Satan has always incited rebellion against God and God's people. Look at Abel and Cain, the one worshipping by faith in the blood, the other by the religion of man's good works. It could be that the Lord had spoken to Cain through Abel, who was a prophet. Cain responded by despising the Lord and killing his brother. This first murder was a foretaste of spiritual warfare down through the ages even to this present day.

We can see spiritual warfare in the choosing of Abraham, Isaac, Jacob, and the establishment of Israel. No doubt Satan was working through Pharaoh during the years of Israel's captivity and it was spiritual warfare when Moses withstood Pharaoh in the Exodus and the Passover. It is interesting to note that it was not Moses' rebuke of Pharaoh, nor the unity of the elect that gave Israel's victory. It was the Word of God and the Blood of the Lamb that defeated Satan. And after defeating their enemies, Israel did not "press in to take the land" of Egypt. They forsook it to head for a better country, one that the Lord had promised them.

We see biblical spiritual warfare taking place through Joshua and his conquest of the promised land; through the book of Judges; during the time of the kings, and even into the Captivity. In fact, some of the greatest victories were made during the Captivity, which underscores the fact that God is waging His war with or without our cooperation.

Daniel 4:34-35 And at the end of the days, I Nebuchadnezzar lifted up mine eyes unto heaven, and mine understanding returned unto me, and I blessed the most High, and I praised and honoured him that liveth for ever, whose dominion is an everlasting dominion, and his kingdom is from generation to generation: And all the inhabitants of the earth are reputed as nothing: and he doeth according to his will in the army of heaven, and among the inhabitants of the earth: and none can stay his hand, or say unto him what doest thou?

It was in Babylon that God revealed his might through Nebuchadnezzar, a pagan king, to the greatest empire the world had ever seen – from Ethiopia to India! Before I even get into the "How's" of spiritual warfare it is important to me to stress this fact, that God is sovereign. It's His war, He wages it! It may please Him to use us in some aspect, but He doesn't need us. His purposes will stand. His counsel cannot be frustrated.

Isaiah 46:9-10 *Remember the former things of old: for I am God, and there is none else; I am God, and there is none like me. Declaring the end from the beginning, and from ancient times the things that are not yet done, saying, My counsel shall stand, and I will do all my pleasure.*

The Sovereignty of God

What do I mean when I talk about the sovereignty of God? I admit that until about five years ago, I did not really believe in a truly sovereign God. Through the Word, He began to reveal this attribute to me. My concept of God was too small. I truly believe this is quite common among Pentecostals. We all need a good dose of the sovereignty of God!

By sovereign, I am referring to several things. A sovereign is answerable to no one. When kings take that title they flatter themselves. No man is a sovereign. Nebuchadnezzar thought he was sovereign for a while until God, in whose hands his life was held, took his mind away from him for seven years. That's right! Nebuchadnezzar was the most powerful political ruler the earth had ever seen. Nations did tremble at his feet and one decision of his could make or break a nation. But, every breath he took was up to God! He didn't realize it, but he was totally dependent on God! When God took his mind away and banished him to live like an animal out in the open fields, there was nothing that he nor anyone else could do about it! You could have cast the spirit of insanity out of him, anointed him with oil, had city-wide prayer or whatever you want, but it would do no good. For the sovereign God had decreed it! And when the set time had come, his mind was given back to him by God. Even more miraculously, his throne was given back as well, having been preserved for him by God, while he grazed out in the field for seven years!

This whole incident took place, *That men may know that the Most High rules in the kingdom of men and gives it to whomsoever He will and sets up over it the basest of men.*"(Daniel 4:17). Nebuchadnezzar had this testimony sent out to all his empire, according to Daniel 4:1, *Unto all people, nations and languages, that dwell in the earth.* Thus he began extending the gospel to all the known world, through that one incident!

God can do more in five minutes than man could ever do in a million lifetimes! God rules. He is sovereign. He needs no one, but we desperately depend on Him, whether we acknowledge Him or not. Billions of years before we were in existence, He was at peak joy! He didn't create us because He was lonely. He has always lived in community, with himself. He is complete! As Acts 17 teaches:

Acts 17:24-25 *God that made the world and all things therein, seeing that he is Lord of heaven and earth, dwelleth not in temples made with hands; Neither is worshipped with men's hands, as though he needed any thing, seeing he giveth to all life, and breath, and all things.*

We don't prop up Him or His cause, He sustains us. On the other hand, every breath you and I take is because of Him. This is what Christians need to recover a belief in a sovereign, independent God, who can't be thwarted, can never be put in debt an Almighty

67

Creator who laughs at the plans of the enemy amassed against "the Lord and his Christ." (Psalm 2)

The Early Church Worshipped a Despot

When the devil tried to intimidate the early Church in Acts 4, they responded with spiritual warfare, but not by attacking "religious spirits", "control", or "Jezebel". They appealed to God "with one accord" and said, "Lord you are God (not the high priests) which hast made the heaven and the earth and the sea and all that in them is." Now, why do you think they appealed to God that way in the time of crisis? They called upon God as creator, God as Lord indeed! In fact, the Greek word Lord is δεσποτης despotes. God as Despot!! Absolute Ruler!! It puts it all back in perspective.

When the Church is being intimidated and harassed, which is the better perspective of those listed below?

Perspective A. The apostles gather the church together and say, "The chief priests and Pharisees and Sadducees have threatened us to stop preaching. But, we are Christians and we have rights too. Let's get our Christian lawyers and fight this in a court of law. We need volunteers to write letters to the Sanhedrin..."

Perspective B. The apostles gather the church together and say, "The chief priests and Pharisees and Sadducees have threatened us to stop preaching in the name of Jesus. But, I know a religious spirit when I see it, and Church we are in warfare. Jezebel we come against you in the name of..(and so on)." It's all up to us Church!

Perspective C. The apostles gather the church together and say, "The chief priests and Sadducees have threatened us to stop preaching in the name of Jesus. But, let's take it to God, our God, creator of heaven and earth, creator of Herod and Pilate."

Acts 4:24-31 And when they heard that, they lifted up their voice to God with one accord, and said, Lord thou art God, which hast made heaven, and earth, and the sea, and all that in them is; who by the mouth of thy servant David hast said, Why did the heathen rage, and the people imagine vain things? The kings of the earth stood up, and the rulers were gathered together against the Lord, and against his Christ. For of a truth against thy holy child Jesus, whom thou hast anointed, both Herod, and Pontius Pilate, with the Gentiles, and the people of Israel, were gathered together, For to do **whatsoever thy hand and thy counsel determined before to be done.** *And now, Lord, behold their threatening: and grant unto thy servants, that with all boldness they may speak thy word, By stretching forth thine hand to heal; and that signs and wonders may be done by the name of thy holy child Jesus. And when they had prayed, the place was shaken where they were assembled together; and they were all filled with the Holy Ghost, and they spoke the word of God with boldness.*

The question is not, who are We? As in, we're Christians, we've got rights too. We can play just as tough as the world does, we've got lawyers, and so forth.

Nor is it, who is the devil? This must be a spirit of intimidation, let's fight him, let's make war in the heavenlies, we are conquerors. Satan, we rebuke you! We are warriors!

The real question is, who is God? The early Church reminded themselves of who their God really was, when they cried out, "Sovereign (Despotes), you are Lord which made heaven and earth and the sea and all that in them is."

They then proceeded to refer in prayer to Psalm 2, a Psalm which I believe will have an increasingly apt application for western Christians in the days to come. I believe that our time at bat is coming. All who will live godly in Christ Jesus will suffer persecution. Christians all over the world suffer for worshipping Jesus. We western Christians, in our ease and comfort, have been the exception and not the rule. As it is written, *Every sacrifice shall be salted with salt.* In other words, all worship shall be costly (Mark 9:49b). The early Church turned to the God of Psalm 2 who laughs at the ragings of the kings of this earth. He doesn't recognize man's sovereignty. He has appointed His own king, Jesus. This king rules from His holy hill, Zion. The plans of earthly rulers are doomed to futility. They want to throw off God's bondages, and cast them away, as it shows in Psalm 2. In other words, they want a self-ruled, autonomous, humanity, a Millennium, without Christ.

However, God has decreed their times, seasons, and spheres of influence. Nations won't be "Christianized" until the sovereign, Christ Jesus, rules them with a rod of iron. In the meantime, we bring the message of Psalm 2:10-13, which is worship Jesus while there is time and receive the blessing of trusting Him, salvation. We can know the fear of God and the joy of the Lord at the same time, through receiving the Son of God, King Jesus. It's all there in Psalm 2. Read it and familiarize yourself with it. Learn spiritual warfare from Psalms 2 and Acts 4!

True spiritual warfare starts with an appreciation for the God we worship. God is sovereign.

Psalm 75:4-10 *I said unto the fools, deal not foolishly: and to the wicked, Lift not up the horn: Lift not up your horn on high: speak not with a stiff neck. For promotion cometh neither from the east, nor from the west, nor from the south. But God is the judge: he putteth down one, and setteth up another. For in the hand of the Lord there is a cup, and the wine is red; it is full of mixture; and he poureth out of the same: but the dregs thereof, all the wicked of the earth shall wring them out, and drink them. But I will declare for ever; I will sing praises to the God of Jacob. All the horns of the wicked also will I cut off; but the horns of the righteous shall be exalted.*

Sometimes I think we act like we don't believe this! God says "I put down, I build up." We think it is our job to bring down. But God understands how and when to act, we do not. Realize this: God uses Satan. Definitely! God uses Satan! If he had no use for him do you think he would be around? God is not putting down Satan and his strongholds because He is using them, in His divine plan. I think Spiritual Warfare teachers are unknowingly rebelling against the plan of God!

God Is Still The Sovereign Lord of History

Do you honestly believe Satan has some legal hold on God as some spuriously teach? Do you believe that God lost control of His creation after Adam sinned, and had to bargain with Satan to buy it back? What a travesty of biblical truth that is!

The Roman, Greek, Babylonian, and Persian empires were all ungodly, antichrist expressions. But, God allowed them to survive and even to expand and prosper! Why? He used them to prepare the world for Christ's coming. The Babylonians were essential in God's plan, for He used them to scatter reluctant, missionary Israel from Ethiopia to India. He also used them to destroy Israel's temple, thus necessitating the development of synagogues in every community of any size in the Babylonian Empire! So, by the time of Christ, Moses was preached in every city of the known world and every synagogue was packed not only with Jews, but God fearing Gentiles and proselytes, circumcised Gentile converts to Judaism. Watch out, God's purpose will stand! If you are called to be a missionary, you will be a missionary one way or the other, who were willingly or unwillingly. The God of the Bible is a Sovereign who works all things together to fulfil the counsel of His good pleasure:

Ephesians 1:11 *In whom also we have obtained an inheritance, being predestinated according to the purpose of him who worketh all things after the counsel of his own will:*

How did God use the Medo-Persian Empire? It was Cyrus the king, a pagan Gentile, whom God named at least 100 years before his birth as the one who would fulfil His purposes.

Isaiah 44:24-45:6 *Thus saith the Lord, thy redeemer, and he that formed thee from the womb, I am the Lord that maketh all things; that stretcheth forth the heavens alone; that spreadeth abroad the earth by myself; That frustrateth the tokens of the liars, and maketh diviners mad; that turneth wise men backward, and maketh their knowledge foolish; That confirmeth the word of his* *servant, and performeth the counsel of his messengers; that saith to Jerusalem, Thou shalt be inhabited; and to the cities of Judah, Ye shall be built, and I will raise up the decayed places thereof; That saith to the deep, Be dry, and I will dry up thy rivers;* **That saith of Cyrus, He is my shepherd, and shall perform all my pleasure; even saying to Jerusalem, Thou shalt be built; and to the temple, Thy foundation shall be laid.** *Thus saith the Lord to his anointed, to Cyrus, whose right hand I have holden, to subdue nations before him; and I will loose the loins of kings, to open before him the two leaved gates; and the gates shall not be shut; I will go before thee, and make the crooked places straight; I will break in pieces the gates of brass, and cut in sunder the bars of iron; And I will give thee the treasures of darkness, and hidden riches of secret places that thou mayest know that I, the Lord, which call thee by thy name, am the God of Israel. For Jacob my servant's sake, Israel mine elect, I have even called thee by thy name; I have surnamed thee, though thou hast not known me. I am the Lord, and there is none else, there is no God beside me; I girded thee, though thou hast not known me; That they may know from the rising of the sun, and from the west, that there is none beside me, I am the Lord, and there is none else.*

What did Cyrus do? He gave the decree that Israel should go back to the Holy Land from their captivity, and He financed the rebuilding of the temple and walls of Jerusalem. The man didn't even know God, but God used him! Does God need Christians? No, but it pleases Him to allow us a small portion of the work of redemption. The Persians and Medes had to overthrow the Babylonian empire to be able to release the holy people from captivity. A staggering feat to man, but nothing to God! There had to be a temple in Israel into which Christ would come, to fulfil prophecy. God used Cyrus to bring Israel back, and finance the rebuilding of the temple.

God also used the Greeks. Out of nowhere, Alexander the Great rose up from a tiny, backwater nation, and in twelve short, furious years, conquered the whole known world! This was God's unique plan! Was Alexander Christian? No, he was somewhat of an antichrist. He tried to form a one world government, tried to mix the populations, and bring the whole world under one culture. So, how did God use him? God had him enforce the learning of Greek language upon the peoples of his realm. Koine, or common Greek, became the lingua franca of the whole known world. How did this fulfil God's purposes? When Christ came into the world with the gospel, preaching advanced rapidly because there were virtually no language barriers from Ethiopia to India and even up into Europe. Our God is awesome! Finally we come to Rome, the one Daniel describes as the most brutal empire of all. What a Godless place Rome was. The emperors were worshipped as "saviours of the world". Their official messages were called gospels and many of them came to believe they were gods. Could God use them? Certainly, much in every way! How big is your God? Rome crushed Greece. Alexander was like a shooting star, very short-lived, for God was through with Him! Rome actually "paved" the way for the gospel. Roman roads literally connected every major city. The Roman military cleared the roads of bandits. The Roman navy destroyed the pirates that swarmed the Mediterranean, making sea travel safe. With those improvements alone, Rome paved the way for the greatest time of universal prosperity, travel, and interchange the world had ever known. I won't even go into the Roman census God used, (see Luke 2), and the Roman cross. As Psalm 2 says, the kings of the earth can plot, plan, and conspire all they want but the bottom line is they are going to fulfil God's plan.

Not one jot or tittle of God's purpose can fail! By the time the first evangelists went out with news of the good gospel of God, they travelled on Roman roads protected by legionnaires; spoke Koine Greek, they had a Greek Bible; testified of the Messiah who had appeared suddenly in a rebuilt temple; and headed first to synagogues in every major city of the world, where the earliest churches were composed of Gentile proselytes and God-fearers, and a scattering of synagogue Jews! Hallelujah!! God prepared the way. And He used the very satanic kingdoms that today's Church is determined to overthrow by spiritual warfare. How little they understand of the purposes of God.

What It Means to Worship the Sovereign God

Psalm 115:1-3 *Not unto us, O Lord, not unto us, but unto thy name give glory, for thy mercy, and for thy truth's sake. Wherefore should the heathen say, Where is now their God? But our God is in the heavens; he hath done whatsoever he hath pleased.*

As a sovereign, God always does what He pleases. He is never obliged to do anything. He knows of no necessity. He didn't have to save you and me. No one can ever put Him in debt.

Romans 11:35-36 *Or who hath first given to him, and it shall be recompensed unto him again? For of him, and through him, and to him, are all things: to whom be glory forever.*

Who can ever say, "God I did this, you have to do that?" God forbid. Fortunately for us, it pleases Him to save us. God wants to save, for He is good, full of mercy. This is brought out in Matthew 20:1-15.

Matthew 20:1-15 *For the kingdom of heaven is like unto a man that is an householder, which went out early in the morning to hire labourers into his vineyard. And when he had agreed with the labourers for a penny a day, he sent them into his vineyard. And he went out about the third hour, and saw others standing idle in the marketplace. And said unto them; Go ye also into the vineyard, and whatsoever is right I will give you. And they went their way. Again he went out about the sixth and ninth hour, and did likewise. And about the eleventh hour he went out, and found others standing idle, and saith unto them, why stand ye here all the day idle? They say unto him, Because no man hath hired us. He saith unto them,. Go ye also into the vineyard; and whatsoever is right, that shall ye receive. So when even was come, the lord of the vineyard saith unto his steward, Call the labourers, and give them their hire, beginning from the last unto the first. And when they came that were hired about the eleventh hour they received every man a penny. But when the first came, they supposed that they should have received more;*

and they likewise received every man a penny. And when they had received it, they murmured against the good man of the house, saying These last have wrought but one hour, and thou hast made them equal unto us, which have borne the burden and heat of the day. But he answered one of them, and said, Friend, I do thee no wrong; didn't not thou agree with me for a penny? Take that thine is, and go thy way: I will give unto this last, even as unto thee. Is it not lawful for me to do what I will with mine own? Is thine eye evil, because I am good?

Obviously God didn't hire the man in the last hour because He needed another man. The reason He hired him was because the labourer needed work. We are the needy ones. God saves us because we need salvation. What of the labourer who demanded more? Well, the moral of this story is, no people will ever receive less then justice, but some will receive more, grace. As Daniel wrote in Daniel 4:34-35, no one can say to God, what are you doing? As it is written:

Romans 9:15 *For he saith to Moses, I will have mercy on whom I will have mercy, and I will have compassion on who I will have compassion.*

How then did we even come to know God? "Well I found the Lord back in 1977", you say. Don't flatter yourself. You didn't find the Lord because you weren't looking for Him. Romans 3 isn't kidding when it says "There is none that seeks after God." You were running from God when He sought you out, found you, revealed Himself to you, gave you faith to believe, destroyed all your arguments of self-justification, and gave you salvation. There are no earnest seekers after truth who "just haven't found God yet."

Luke 10:21-22 *In that hour Jesus rejoiced in spirit, and said, I thank thee, O Father, Lord of Heaven and earth, that thou hast hid these things from the wise and prudent, and hast revealed them unto babes; even so, Father; for so it seemed good in thy sight. All things* *are delivered to me of my Father; and no man knoweth who the Son is, but the Father, and who the Father is, but the Son and he to whom the Son will reveal him.*

You wouldn't know God at all if He hadn't revealed Himself to you. There is no way you could and you wouldn't even want to, if you could. Man isn't seeking after God. He isn't just groping in the dark, trying to find Him through drugs, sex, alcohol, false religions, and any other spurious, soul-destroying route. Man is suppressing what he knows is true of God and running from God!

Romans 1:19-25 *Because that which may be known of God is manifest in them; for God hath shewed it unto them. For the invisible things of him from the creation of the world are clearly seen, being understood by the things that are made, even his eternal power and Godhead; so that they are without excuse: because that, when they knew God, they glorified him not as God, neither were thankful; but became vain in their imaginations, and their foolish heart was darkened. Professing themselves to be wise, they became fools, and changed the glory of the incorruptible God into an image made like to corruptible man, and to birds, and four footed beasts, and creeping things. Wherefore God also gave them up to uncleanness through the lusts of their own hearts, to dishonour their own bodies between themselves; Who changed the truth of God into a lie, and worshipped and served the creature more than the Creator, who is blessed for ever. Amen.*

Romans 1:28 *And even as they did not like to retain God in their knowledge, God gave them over to a reprobate mind, to do those things which are not convenient.*

Men and women really don't like to think about God. Why do I press this point so much in a discussion of the sovereignty of God? It is crucial to see that the way you perceive this issue has affected the way you perceive everything else in the spirit. Either you have a God-centered perspective or a man-centered one. Jesus tells me that

I didn't choose him, He chose me. It's not, "God, bless my program." It's, "God, what is your program?" If it is really true that you found God after seeking Him, then you took the initiative. You did it! But if, as the Bible reports, God revealed Himself to you, even when you were rejecting Him, then God took the initiative. He loved us first. Don't get me wrong, I do believe some people get to the point where it seems they are seeking God, but only because God put it in their heart to do it.

John 15:16 *Ye have not chosen me, but I have chosen you, and ordained you, that ye should go and bring forth fruit, and that your fruit should remain: that whatsoever ye shall ask of the Father in my name, he may give it you.*

John 6:44 *No man can come to me, except the Father which hath sent me draw him: and I will raise him up at the last day.*

Joseph had a secure, God-centered faith that sustained him through many injustices perpetrated by first his brothers and then Potiphar's wife. Instead of waging political or spiritual warfare for thirteen years, fighting for his rights, he committed himself to God who works all things together for good, to those who love Him and are called according to His purpose. Joseph was realistic enough to see there was a human reason for his dilemma. But he never counted the depravity of his brothers or the treachery of Potiphar's wife as bigger than God. "You meant it for evil but God meant it for good!" Nothing happens that God doesn't either decree or allow to happen.

It is for this reason that Peter can hold the men who crucified Jesus responsible for that act, but on the other hand, can say:

Acts 2:23-24 *Him, being delivered by the determinate counsel and foreknowledge of God, ye have taken, and by wicked hands have crucified and slain: Whom God hath raised up, having loosed the pains of death: because it was not possible that he should be holden of it.*

The foundation for true spiritual warfare is faith in a mighty, loving God. I could expound on any number of attributes of God, but the particular need for us is a knowledge of the sovereign, benevolent despot, the God of the Bible.

2 Chronicles 20:6 And said, O Lord God of our fathers, art not thou God in heaven? And rulest not thou over all the kingdoms of the heathen? And in thine hand is there not power and might, so that no man is able to withstand thee?

7

Your Adversary And His Strategy

Keep To Your Boundaries

I Peter 5:8-10 Be sober, be vigilant; because your adversary the devil, as a roaring lion, walketh about, seeking whom he may devour; Whom resist steadfast in the faith, knowing that the same afflictions are accomplished in your brethren that are in the world. But the God of all grace, who hath called us unto his eternal glory by Christ Jesus, after that ye have suffered a while, make you perfect, stablish, strengthen, settle you.

The foundation for spiritual warfare is faith in the sovereign God! Now, let's proceed to a discussion about our adversary in warfare, Satan and his host. From this scripture we can see that we are not dealing with dualism. Dualism is the pagan idea that God and Satan are equal but opposite forces, and whomever we champion will prevail, either short or long term. People in the Christian community don't doubt for one minute that ultimately God will prevail, but they don't act like it in the short run. There is a practical dualism at work, even if not as a conscious theology. The idea is that, if we don't do something about it, Satan will triumph.

Settle it once and for all, Jesus is Lord. His purposes can't be thwarted. His counsel will stand! The text tells us that our adversary, Satan, has to roam about (he's not omnipresent), seeking (he's not omniscient), whomsoever he can devour (he's not omnipotent)! We are dealing with a created being, created by God, fulfilling God's purposes, though unwillingly, of course. As a created being, our adversary is subject to many limitations. Anything he has at all has been "given" to him by God "for a season". "Jesus, are you come to torment us before the time?", cry the demons that Jesus exorcised. They knew their ultimate defeat was at hand.

Satan has been cast down to the earth. He is full of great wrath, knowing his time is short. The point is, Satan, demons, angels, Christians, and sinners all are created beings and can only operate within the measure God has given them. There is a prescribed measure, a boundary line, that God has ordained for all of his creation. The waters of the ocean and the floods have been given a line. The Creator has said, "This far and no farther." Trees don't walk, mud doesn't sing, all creation has a measure. If Satan tries anything, in general, it is to tempt, or deceive man into going beyond or outside his "measure". Satan's original sin was his desire to "go beyond the measure":

Isaiah 14:12-15 How art thou fallen from heaven, O Lucifer, son of the morning! How art thou cut down to the ground, which didst weaken the nations! For thou hast said in thine heart, I will ascend into heaven, I will exalt my throne above the stars of God; I will sit also upon the mount of the congregation, in the sides of the north; I will ascend above the heights of the clouds; I will be like the most High. Yet thou shalt be brought down to hell, to the sides of the pit.

Not content with remaining within the boundaries God had set for him, he transgressed, and crossed the line. Iniquity (lawlessness = no boundaries) was found in his heart and he fell. The Bible speaks of the angels who sinned, who left their first state, in the days of Noah, being bound in chains for the Judgment. Leaving your measure, your God-given boundaries, always invokes swift judgement. Adam and Eve also, tempted and deceived, left their God-given boundary, in a failed attempt to "be like gods", "knowing good and evil", making their own judgments. Attempting to leave God-given measures, in an effort to gain more freedom, always leaves you even more bound than before. Promising them liberty, Peter says by the Holy Ghost, they themselves are slaves of corruption. Freedom is only found within the measure in which God created you to operate.

Another example of this is King Saul, who was not content to wait, as God instructed him, for the priest to offer the sacrifice before battle. Why? He could see the enemy was gaining an advantage! He thought, "We have to do something now!" With that kind of discontent, Saul left his God-given measure as a king and entered the priestly role, presumptuously, to offer the sacrifice himself. He had made his own assessment of the situation and acted accordingly. No wonder he lost the kingdom.

In the same manner, though, many are making their own judgement of the spiritual scene as well and acting presumptuously. What exactly are the parameters in which the "Church militant" is to operate? Are we to engage the principalities directly, identifying them, counter-strategizing them? Or should we act indirectly, petitioning God all the more, evangelizing the lost, refuting Satan's lies to the people he has deceived? Are we to "make war in the heavenlies" or are we the earthly "mop up force"? These are valid questions that need to be raised. I am sure Saul was quite zealous to win the Lord's battle, but that was no excuse for his presumption.

II Peter 2:10-12 *But chiefly them that walk after the flesh in the lust of uncleanness, and despise government. Presumptuous are they, self-willed, they are not afraid to speak evil of dignities. Whereas angels, which are greater in power and might, bring not railing accusation against them before the Lord. But these, as natural brute beasts, made to be taken and destroyed, speak evil of the things that they understand not; and shall utterly perish in their own corruption.*

Jude 8-10 *Likewise also these filthy dreamers defile the flesh, despise dominion, and speak evil of dignities. Yet Michael the* *archangel, when contending with the devil he disputed about the body of Moses, durst not bring against him a railing accusation, but said, The Lord rebuke thee. But these speak evil of those things which they know not; but what they know naturally, as brute beasts, in those things they corrupt themselves.*

The angels of God never transgress, or step out of their assigned sphere, not even in their confrontation with Satan. It is always, "The Lord rebuke you Satan." Angels know their strength is in the power of His might.

A more orthodox view of spiritual warfare would be an indirect one. I know this is not popular with our confrontational culture. But, what does the Bible teach? What did the apostles do?

The heavenly realms are not our assignment. The Great Commission is not, "Go into all the world and bring down principalities and focus on defeating Satan." We need to be extremely careful before God in keeping to our "measure" or God-given boundaries. Part of Satan's strategy has always been to tempt man to exceed his limitations. He incites us to transgress, to be discontent operating in the sphere in which God placed us.

Indirect warfare means acknowledging the struggle against principalities, powers, and rulers of the darkness of this age. The nature of the indirect warfare struggle takes three different postures. One, striving to pray to God, through demonic opposition; two, reaching the men that demons have deceived, in spite of hindrances; and three, standing against the demonic realm, of course, casting them out when called for.

It is actually Satan who has tempted Charismatics especially, to go after him directly, using warring prayer, and identifying strongmen, and so forth. Satan waves the red cloth of the matador, and the bull is obediently charging, but to what effect? Daniel prophesied that in the last days, Satan would make war on the saints to "wear them down". Is this just one attempt to do so?

But, the orthodox view of spiritual warfare is prevailing prayer to God, not interaction with demons. It is prayer to God that brings true revival and blessing upon our efforts, and brings anointed preaching that specifically addresses the deception of the day, all in spite of Satanic opposition. When Paul had a messenger of Satan buffet him repeatedly, he cried out to God for a removal of the demon three times. God's reply was instructive, "My grace is sufficient for you, for my power is made perfect in weakness!" God didn't "name the strongman" for Paul nor teach him how to seek for the historical and psychological roots of his troubling spirit. God simply told Paul to depend on His grace all the more. God is able to turn men from darkness to light, and from the power of Satan to salvation, instructing them how to receive remission of sin.

Acts 26:15-18 And I said, Who art thou, Lord? And he said, I am Jesus whom thou persecutest. But rise, and stand upon thy feet; for I have appeared unto thee for this purpose, to make thee a minister and a witness both of these things which thou hast seen, and of those things in the which I will appear unto thee; Delivering thee from the people, and from the Gentiles, unto whom now I send thee. To open their eyes, and to turn them from darkness to light, and from the power of Satan unto God, that they may receive forgiveness of sins, and inheritance among them which are sanctified by faith that is in me.

What is our God-given measure? It is laid out for us in the Word of God. We are to go into all the world and preach the Gospel to all creatures. We are to offer prayer and intercession for all men, especially those who are in authority. We are to build up one another, speaking the truth in love. We are also to hold forth the Word of Life in the midst of a wicked and perverted generation. Our measure also includes casting out devils from individuals and healing sick individuals through faith in the name of Jesus. We are not to be intimidated by Satan, but to "stand against" him and his lies. Remember that Satan wants you to "go beyond what is written", whether it be to do "good" or evil. I don't see in the Word of God that fighting Satan, identifying his princes, and attacking him directly is part of our measure!

When Jesus was tempted in the desert, in Matthew 4 and Luke 4, Satan revealed his prime strategy. The first temptation was to turn these stones into bread if you are the Son of God. Is there anything wrong with eating after 40 days? Is it written anywhere that you are not to turn stones into bread? The essence of this temptation is two-fold. Number one, self-esteem: Jesus, prove who you are, do something powerful!

Number two, self-will: Jesus, do something in the power of God, out of your own initiative.

In the second temptation, we see Satan offering a compromise. Jesus was tempted to make things happen of Himself, of His own human will. Remember, that Jesus came to receive the kingdoms of this world and make them into the kingdoms of our Lord and of his Christ. Here was a quicker and more effective way to achieve it! "Whatever you've been doing these past 30 years apparently hasn't been working too well, Jesus", Satan says.

In the third temptation, deception is added. "Jesus, I have scripture to claim, that says God **has** to save you if you jump off the temple. He said He would give his angels charge over you, so He has to do it! Think of how spectacular that would be for your ministry! Everyone would see it and then they wouldn't mock the people of God! They'd see that we are mighty warriors!" The same reasoning is now applied to spiritual warfare – we can prove to the world just how effective we are.

In every case, though the temptation tested different areas of human life, the essence was the same. Each test tried to pressure or lure Jesus to do something out of his own initiative. Anything at all, just get some results, Jesus! This was the very opposite of Jesus' submission to the Father's will, in which he said "Of my own self, I do nothing, I only do what I see the Father do". Jesus in John 5 walks out to a crowded porch of sick and heals only one! He then walks away. He would do nothing, not even "good" out of His own initiative. He was obedient to the Father's plan.

Christians are being swamped and pressured with "good". It would be good to protest abortion, it's good to elect Christians to government, to clean up TV, or "wage warfare prayer", and run the devil out of town! It may be good, but my question is, is it within the measure that God has given you? Has God called you to it?

If God "identifies" a spiritual entity to me in prayer, and leads me specifically to address it, then I will say, "The Lord rebuke you Satan for it is written." But, the problem with many Charismatics is that when God speaks a word, we write a sentence. Our "good" has to die as well as our evil, till we come to the point where we can say with the Son of God, "Out of my own initiative, I do nothing." God isn't panicking because of the spots and blemishes in the Church. God isn't wringing His hands in despair that the "devil is winning because the Church just isn't doing her job". For the same reason, Jesus didn't even open his mouth publicly for thirty years. He didn't up and quit carpentry at age twenty because "so many are perishing". He knew that if he would respond to God at the appointed time, and not do it himself under Satanic or human pressure, then God could do more in two minutes than he could do unaided in a thousand years of humanly inspired, powerless "ministry". (How many today are acting on their own initiative and are driven by human concerns about what is "good" and "what needs to be done"?)

Paul was another one who understood the limits of his ministry measure. He never forgot his calling and his God-given mission statement. (Acts 26:15-18) For many of us, the situation would have been different. If we had lived in Paul's day, some of us would have tried to get into the Roman legislature to repeal the slavery laws, or clean up the circus acts. Others would be leading crusades against "Diana of the Ephesians" or writing books about how to bind Zeus! But, Paul just stayed within his measure. His "warfare" was *To turn men from darkness to light, from Satan's power to God, to get them to receive forgiveness of sins and an inheritance.* His weapons were the preaching of truth in love, sincerity, prayer to God, and the name of Jesus to cast out devils.

Despite that, Paul would tell the Thessalonians (I Thessalonians 2:18) that Satan had hindered him again and again from coming to them. Did he go on to boast of how he had given Satan a black eye? No, Paul didn't counter attack Satan directly. He appealed to God.

The idea that we are "locked into direct conflict with Satan, toe to toe" is one of the biggest, most unbiblical deceptions today. Satan may be directly attempting to thwart, hinder, tempt, and deceive us, but our resistance to him is based on "submitting to God", not railing at Satan. We are always to stand our ground, in our position in God. At most it's "The Lord rebuke you Satan", or "It is written...", or even as Psalms 8 and 149 teach, by praising God! You see, it's God's warfare, it's Jesus versus Satan. This present presumption of demonic combat is only setting people up for a massive deception!

As for Satan's particular strategies, we are not to be ignorant of them. (II Corinthians 2:11) Let us summarize them rather concisely. As a created being, Satan has his own limited sphere of influence. He cannot simply tear people to shreds at will. If he could, don't you think we'd all be dead? This power has not been given him by God. All that God has allowed Satan to do, is to incite people through their minds, either to destroy themselves or destroy one another. Satan will do this on an individual basis, or on a family, or a society. But, he has to work with thoughts, cultivating them into ideas, then imaginations, then high thinking that exalts itself against the knowledge of God, until finally impregnable strongholds of deception are formed. This all takes place in the minds of men. The scripture calls Satan the one who deceives the whole world.

As I said, he can't destroy us overtly. But God has given him the ability to use thought and ideas. He tries to plant them in our mind in such a way that we undo ourselves and others. He, Satan, has two allies in his struggle: the world and the flesh. The world, that cosmos, which means "order", "adornment", is the whole society of those who seek to live independently of God. It is opposed to God and hostile to Christ. The world will not receive the Spirit. The flesh, that part of our being which is not born-again, cannot please God, though it often strives to, in its own effort and for its own glory. The flesh can be identified as that part of our nature which is not born-again, the old man who seeks to live independently of Christ.

Ephesians 2:1-3 *And you hath he quickened, who were dead in* *trespasses and sins; wherein in time past ye walked according to the course of this world, according to the prince of the power of the air, the spirit that now worketh in the children of disobedience; among whom also we all had our conversation in times past in the lusts of our flesh, fulfilling the desires of the flesh and of the mind; and were by nature the children of wrath, even as others.*

We lived in "the course of this world. According to the prince of the power of the air. In the lusts of our flesh...the desires of the flesh and the mind."

There you have it! The world, the flesh, and the devil, these have arrayed themselves against the Father, the Son, and the Spirit. The world in particular is opposed to the Father. Those who have "the love of the world", have no room in their hearts for "the love of the Father". The devil is especially opposed to Jesus, who through death, destroyed him who had the power of death, the devil, and delivered those held captive to bondage, through the fear of death. The flesh is the enemy within who is ever opposed to the Holy Spirit. To be fleshly minded is to be at enmity with God. The religion of the flesh is to try to please God through self- effort. Those who "put confidence" in the flesh, always persecute the people of the Spirit.

As has been said, Satan is confined to the mental realm. He has the full co-operation of the world, (they'll print everything he says). And he has the full sympathy of the flesh, to which he continually appeals.

The overall purpose of Satan is two-fold. There is a positive and negative aspect. The positive is, Satan would love to have a Christless Millennium, an era of peace on earth and good will toward men, with harmony, prosperity, and healing, all without God! That's right folks! Satan doesn't want anarchy, mayhem, and destruction, though he will use them. What he really wants is a world of harmony and peace, without bowing the knee to Christ. He would be far better represented by the United Nations or the World Council of Churches, than by the Satanic "Church". The Anti-Christ won't have horns, a long pointy tail, and fangs. He will be a man of peace, sensitivity, and enlightenment, even a man of "compassion".

He will be the embodiment of man without God, man at his highest aspirations and ideals. He will be too pure to worship at a bloodied cross, and even more merciful than God! His religion will have no hell or judgement, but there will be tolerance for all (all, that is, except the dissenters to his religion!). The epic struggle is not the struggle between good and evil, but good and good! What man calls good is not the same as what God calls good. Eve thought it would be good to eat the fruit, and become like God. What's so bad about self-improvement? Remember that Satan doesn't savour the things that be of Satan, (pure, unvarnished evil) he savers the things that be of man, (subtle deceptions and half-truths). (Matthew 16:23) In other words, Satan is more humanistic then he is Satanic, more of a Norman Vincent Peale then he is an Alistair Crowley! Maybe the Antichrist will even institute laws that banish Satanic rites from his lovely new world – that will deceive everyone into thinking he MUST be the Messiah! The whole world is following Satan in a "good" direction. They want to end war, cure disease, and stop hunger. They are seeking tolerance, unity, and love for all, never mind just saving the whales! But, and this is a big but – they want to achieve all this without God, ignoring Christ.

***Psalms 2:1-10** Why do the heathen rage, and the people imagine a vain thing? The kings of the earth set themselves, and the rulers take counsel together, against the Lord, and against his anointed saying, Let us break their bands asunder, and cast away their cords from us. He that sitteth in the heavens shall laugh: the Lord shall have them in derision. Then shall he speak unto them in his wrath, and vex them in his sore displeasure. Yet have I set my king upon my holy hill of Zion. I will declare the decree: the Lord hath said unto me, Thou art my Son; this day have I begotten thee. Ask of me, and I shall give thee the heathen for thine inheritance, and the uttermost parts of the earth for thy possession. Thou shalt break them with a rod of iron; thou shalt dash them in pieces like a potter's vessel. Be wise now therefore, O ye kings; be instructed, ye judges of the earth.*

On the negative side, Satan's purpose is to oppose salvation and nullify the Church. If he can't blind people from salvation, he wants to cancel out their effectiveness as radiant witnesses. He can do this either openly or by persecution, which usually doesn't work too well. Or, as Church history has shown, Satan can infiltrate the Church and divert or distract it into irrelevancy. Just like the bullfighter who waves his red cloth, Satan distracts the Church from its true purpose. He would much rather have you spend your energy on a red rag than have you fulfilling your God-given purpose.

How Does The Kingdom of God Come?

***Colossians 1:13** Who hath delivered us from the power of darkness, and hath translated us into the kingdom of his dear Son.*

Whenever people willingly submit to God, the kingdom of God is established. As the kingdom of God advances, the "kingdom of darkness" recedes. Once again, our focal point should be advancing the kingdom of God, not attacking the kingdom of Satan. The pivotal point is submission to God. Will you submit to God or won't you? It doesn't matter what spirits control you or how, they can't stop you from submitting to God if you want to. Look at the man with the Legion of demons! Even he was able to run to Jesus and bow down and worship him, in a demon-possessed state! Note that this man's deliverance came afterwards. Jesus didn't cast out the Legion to make the demoniac respond. It was the other way around. At the point where someone submits to God and His Word, His kingdom advances that far. At the point where a person digs their heels in and refuses to yield, the kingdom of darkness remains in place!

***James 4:7** Submit yourselves therefore to God. Resist the devil and he will flee from you.*

Note the order, first submit to God, then resist the devil and he will flee from you. The emphasis is submission to God. The verse doesn't say, rebuke the devil, research the devil, fight the devil. It says to resist, withstand, stand against, hold your ground! Our ground is the finished work of Christ and our submission to it. If Satan can convince us that Christ's work is somehow insufficient, and that we must "do something" to add to it, then he has lured us "off our ground" into his arena, the flesh, and there he will beat us up!

II Corinthians 10:3-6 For though we walk in the flesh, we do not war after the flesh; (For the weapons of our warfare are not carnal, but mighty through God to the pulling down of strongholds.) Casting down imaginations, and every high thing that exalteth itself against the knowledge of God, and bringing into captivity every thought to the obedience of Christ; And having in a readiness to revenge all disobedience, when your obedience is fulfilled.

Remember, the focal point of Satan's attack is in the mental realm. That's why I can't emphasize enough that effective spiritual warfare is waged in the world of ideas and philosophies, in order to correct the deceptions. This is not to say that believing prayer is irrelevant. But, even the focus of the prayer can be misguided, as in the matador/bull example. The focus of the believing prayer cannot become primarily Satan and his minions. The Bible never shows Jesus or His followers constantly praying directly at demons. Our prayer focus has to be God, His glory, His purposes, and the people He has paid so dearly to redeem. Spiritual warfare is going out in the anointing of that prayer relationship and confronting the blind with the light of the glorious Gospel of Christ. It involves bringing down vain imaginations and every high speculation that exalts itself against the knowledge of Christ.

Deception – What Is It?

Deception is, first and foremost, the work of Satan. His first success was Adam. The question I would raise, however, is about the human motives for being deceived. What was wrong with Adam and Eve in the first place, that caused them to want to be like God?

The inclination to sin is already in the human heart. I was taught early on, the only person who can be conned is the one who already has crime in his heart.

A typical con operates this way, "Psst, Buddy, let me show you how we can take advantage of the insurance company or the utilities or the government." Whatever the temptation, the basic idea is, "Here's a slick way to get something for nothing!" Well, I don't want anything God didn't give me. Cons appeal to the wrong motives we already have!

Satan couldn't kill Adam and Eve directly. He is limited that way. So he had to teach them to undo themselves. The answer in the Garden wasn't to yell at the devil, as spiritual warfare teaches. Adam should have said, "Eve, what in the world is the matter with us? We are not God, and never can be. We are people made in the image of God, created to worship Him! Let's be content with the way God made us." Eve: "Thanks, Adam. I needed that." Exit snake!

When Satan wanted to destroy Israel, in the days of Balaam, he found he could not because God was protecting them. Balaam told Balak, "We can't destroy these people, God's hand is on them. You can't curse them, so we have to get them to destroy themselves. Send for those pretty Moabite women...". Satan had to present temptation, in order to seduce God's people to condemn themselves by their actions.

James 1:13-15 Let no man say when he is tempted, I am tempted of God; for God cannot be tempted with evil, neither tempteth he any man; but every man is tempted, when he is drawn away of his own lust, and enticed. Then when lust hath conceived, it bringeth forth sin; and sin, when it is finished bringeth forth death.

Satan is also the Accuser. He will accuse God to you, you to God, others to you, you to others, you to yourself. The Greek word for the Devil is Diabolos. It comes from the Greek "to accuse or slander another" – διαβαλλω DIABALLO. This word is composed of δια DIA (through, over or across), and βαλλω

BALLO (to throw). Diabolos, or the Devil, could therefore be translated, "throwing-over". I picture two bowling pins standing side by side, standing firm until the ball is thrown at them. Then they not only fall over, but are divided from each other. They are knocked apart! Satan throws accusing, slanderous thoughts at people that divide them!

For instance: "Eve, God knows that in the day you eat the fruit of the tree, your eyes will be opened and you will be like gods. So, God is holding you back from the good life, right? God is depriving you!"

The result? Adam said to God, "the woman you gave me, she made me sin!" The Devil succeeded both in causing Eve to fall AND sowing separation and accusation between Adam and his wife. He still operates in this way today.

Thus, true spiritual warfare is a matter of overcoming deception, accusation and temptation, on a personal level, and in the wider sphere. The world is deceived. There are certain strongholds of thinking that need to be torn down! Deception is gaining ground even in the Church. God and His people are being accused! People are being mercilessly accused night and day, by Satan, by other people, and inwardly by their own thoughts. Temptation is mowing down many a mighty man and woman. The warfare is intensifying as the time draws near.

Who is it that is tempted and deceived in this way? Anyone can be deceived, especially those who are sure that they are above deception, that is, the proud. The best approach is dependence on God. I have decided that I don't know anything unless God reveals it to me. The choices set before Adam and Eve were the Tree of Life, which was dependence on God, inward wisdom, through an ongoing relationship with Him, and the Tree of Knowledge of Good and Evil, which was independent judgment, and absolute free will, "We decide truth for ourselves."

God said, "if you eat of that fruit, you'll die." Eve looked at it and thought, "It looks good to me. I don't think anything is wrong with eating it. Actually, I think it'll taste good and make me wise." Guess who was right? Eve made her own judgments and died.

Jesus said, "I don't do anything unless I see the Father do it and

I don't know anything unless the Father reveals it. No one knows the Father but the Son, and no one knows the Son unless the Father reveals Him." We are not to make our own judgments, not even about spiritual warfare. We can't know anything about it except what God reveals to us in His Word. For all the insight we have into spiritual things, we are still dependent on an ongoing relationship with God. God shows us what we need to know about spiritual warfare, and nothing more or less. But, Satan has been allowed a short time to deceive. Why? I believe that Satanic deception is God's judgment on a world that rejects "the love of the truth". This is not to say that we shouldn't engage in exposing the deception, by confronting it and tearing down its facade with the "weapons of truth". Like Paul, we are to turn men from darkness to light, from the power of Satan to God, that they may receive forgiveness and an inheritance. Here are some of the ways Satan has deceived the whole world.

1. He tells people what they want to hear anyway. Why did the teaching of evolution sweep the nation? People were already looking for a credible basis to enable them to wash their hands of troublesome thoughts like, original sin, the depravity of man, the final judgement, and the sacrifice of Christ. Science delivered them and offered them the self-created man of evolution! Now their messiah – humanism and reason – has saved them!

2. He exalts a sensual experience above the objective, revealed truth of God. "I know we broke the seventh commandment, but it felt so right and we truly love each other." Or, "I know the Bible teaches one resurrection and then the judgment, but I just know I've had past lives, I've experienced reincarnation, it all came to me in a vision!" It doesn't matter what you have felt or experienced, if it contradicts the Word of God, there is no light in it!

3. He convinces people that their sincerity is a safeguard. "I just know I'm all right, I'm an honest seeker after God." People ignore, to their own peril, scriptures like Jeremiah 17:9, "The heart is deceitful above all things, and desperately wicked: who can know it?" They prefer to "trust their own heart" and lean on their own understanding. It's not enough to have "pure motives". The emphasis has to be trust in the Lord and His Word.

4. Satan wants to imitate the Holy Spirit. One of the strongest books on spiritual warfare I ever have read is called **War on the Saints**, by Jesse Penn-Lewis. This book was written in part also by Evan Roberts. Both Penn-Lewis and Roberts were key leaders of the Welsh Revival of 1904-1906. In the book, she chronicles the counter-move of deceptive spiritual activity that came immediately after the revival. She covers deceptive ideas such as the mistaken location of God, as either inside the believer – ("If Christ is in me, do I pray to Him within myself?" Obviously not) or, as a felt presence in the room. What is the true location of God? Christ is at the right hand of God, in the heavenly realm, interceding for us. We direct our thoughts and prayers there, uniting with God by faith and through Jesus. At the same time, Christ by His Spirit indwells us individually and corporately as the Body. But no individual Christian has God wholly within him.

This book also warns of "waiting on the Spirit." What does that mean? When it means being passive, blanking out the mind, and waiting to hear inner voices, it is an open door to deceiving spirits!

Or, man can hear a counterfeit voice of God. God's voice is heard and known in the spirit of a man. He also speaks to us through the conscience and through His written Word, but demonic voices can be heard whispering suggestions to the mind. These voices accuse, torment, urge ridiculous and hasty acts, or suggest that "you are special – you will have a global ministry" and so on, exalting the flesh. These voices also give false predictions. Satan takes advantage of sincere people, even the most devout and keen, especially in the areas above mentioned. There are many voices in the world and none without significance.

I Timothy 4:1-3 Now the Spirit speaketh expressly, that in the latter times some shall depart from the faith, giving heed to seducing spirits, and doctrines of devils; Speaking lies in hypocrisy; having their conscience seared with a hot iron; Forbidding to marry, and commanding to abstain from meats, which God hath created to be received with thanksgiving of them which believe and know the truth.

Everything must be tested by the Word!

There are many deceptions similar to the ones above being promoted in the Charismatic world today. They are not new! At the time of the Welsh revival, people were being led astray by counterfeit visions, feelings and sensations, gusts of wind, scents, ministering angels, outbursts of laughter, groaning, and rolling around on the floor.

People are eager to grasp ideas that would make them a "victim" instead of a sinner. Your condition is not caused by your sin, but by other people, and you need psychological reconstruction to rebuild your broken life! Or, there is the teaching that would give man all power and authority, instead of Christ – the Church becomes the Ruler and Judge, not the Lord Jesus! Deceptions abound that exalt man or that absolve man of his culpability before God. How about all the "I went to heaven" stories or, "I went to hell"? Do they square with Luke 16:27-31?

Luke 16:27-31 *Then he said, I pray thee therefore father, that thou wouldest send him to my father's house. For I have five brethren, that he may testify unto them, lest they also come into this place of torment. Abraham saith unto him, they have Moses and the prophets; let them hear them. And he said, nay, father Abraham: but if one return from the dead, they will repent. And he said unto him, if they hear not Moses and the prophets, neither will they be persuaded, though one rose from the dead.*

II Timothy 4:3-4 *For the time will come when they will not endure sound doctrine; but after their own lusts shall they heap to themselves teachers, having itching ears; and they shall turn away their ears from the truth, and shall be turned unto fables.*

Satan recognizes this sinful tendency in man and capitalizes on it. There is a lie for everyone. Lies to justify self, or exalt self, lies that debase God, and bring Him to the level of man. But, as a general rule, there are only two great themes in the world today.

These are spiritual principles that underlie every mode of thinking in the world today. One is called the mystery of godliness (I Timothy 3:16), which can be summarized thus: God had to descend to earth to save sinful man. God became man. He had to condescend to save us. This is the true doctrine of Christ. The other way of thinking is called the mystery of iniquity. That amounts to the exact opposite. That is, self can be exalted above God, man can ascend, we can save ourselves, we can be "as gods." (II Thess. 2:4,7) In one way or the other the whole world and indeed part of the "Church" embraces the second philosophy, rejecting the first. The whole world is deceived by it! I hear it espoused in the Church when I hear things like, "We are going to take over whole nations", or "We've got the power", or "Nations are going to tremble before us." Remember that the boastful pride of life is one of the three essences of worldliness.

I John 2:15-17 Love not the world, neither the things that are in the world. If any man love the world, the love of the Father is not in him. For all that is in the world, the lust of the flesh, and the lust of the eyes, and the pride of life, is not of the Father, but is of the world. And the world passeth away, and the lust thereof; but he that doeth the will of God abideth for ever.

Deception has been defined by one preacher as, "The imposing of false ideas upon a person, which leaves him helpless and vulnerable." It is usually quite difficult to get "undeceived." It is a humiliation to admit that we have been "sold a bill of goods." No one wants to think of themselves as gullible. But, we are dealing with an adversary who has had thousands of years of experience in dealing with the human soul. He is slick, cunning, and disarming. It takes equal doses of truth and love to see someone through, till truth breaks in upon the mind.

Deliverance from deception has to start with doubt. Not all doubt is wrong. God wants Christians to make critical distinctions everyday, and to judge all things and hold fast to what is good. If there is a fear even to question a spiritual experience or standing, then that fear in and of itself is a sign of deception. Every valid teaching and experience of God can stand up to the stiffest scrutiny. I used to run in what would be called "Word of Faith" circles. One man wrote a book questioning the "faith message" and the leadership refused to discuss any of their beliefs and practices with this man. They also told their own followers, don't read that message of unbelief, it will damage your spirit! Any "faith" that must be protected from scriptural examination or others' scrutiny is not real faith. Look at the Bereans. They doubted Paul, and insisted on checking everything out by the Word of God. And Paul questioned the salvation of the Corinthians. There are times when a little doubt can be good, as long as it presses you to God and His Word. It all goes wrong when a person entertains the idea that he is "infallible," above deception, and more advanced in the Spirit than the rest. He is either in deception already, or headed there.

Admitting to the possibility of deception is a huge step in the right direction.

***Ephesians 4:18** Having the understanding darkened, being alienated from the life of God through the ignorance that is in them, because of the blindness of their heart.*

Let's face it, there is a tremendous inclination toward deception in the human race, because of the fall. Deceiving spirits are at work in the world today. The best, safest position is to know yourself in the light of scripture, as a sinner, vulnerable, weak, needing God. Go ahead and re-evaluate every spiritual experience you ever had! Is it biblical? Did it glorify God? Jesus even told his disciples, "Take heed that no man deceive you." If they who walked with Jesus could be deceived, how much more can we?

It is in this area that certain Christian media personalities are truly hurting God's Church. They will not judge anyone at all in the Christian world, except so-called "heresy hunters". Anyone who questions another minister's teaching is a heresy hunter. This is a time where we are to be alert and think critically. And yet, millions are being disarmed by Christian leaders, in the name of love and unity. Doctrine is a dirty word now. "Doctrines divide! I'm not here to preach doctrine, I'm here to 'share' Jesus." Isn't that sweet? Doctrine is the body of truth! Unity is not to be based solely on love, but it is called the unity of the faith! Faith is not a metaphysical force, as some false teachers are promoting today. Faith has moral content, and it is based on certain truths.

Division isn't always bad. Paul said divisions MUST come, to distinguish the true believers from the false:

1 Cor 11:18-19 For first of all, when you come together as a church, I hear that there are divisions among you, and in part I believe it. For there must also be factions among you, that those who are approved may be recognized among you.

Aren't you glad for the Reformation? If it hadn't been for the division with the Roman Church, we would all still be Catholics. We might never have heard about justification by faith. Just because I am calling into question certain teachings does not mean that I am of the accuser of the brethren. It is time for Christian leadership to rise up and speak against this nonsense. It is time for some real leadership to arise with moral courage, to call black, black and white, white.

If "every denomination that calls on the name of Jesus is Christian," then being a Christian doesn't mean anything. Does infant baptism save? Can you create reality with mind power? Is Robert Schuller right when he calls for a New Reformation of Self-Esteem? Should we pray to Mary? If everything is all right except criticism, then we are in dire straits! Then, there are no longer any distinctions. Why not bring in the Mormons and Jehovah's Witnesses? We have a real discernment crisis on our hands.

I would recommend confused Christians to read these books:

War on the Saints, by Jesse Penn-Lewis
Satan's Devices, by Robert Morey
The Seduction of Christianity, by David Hunt
Love Not the World, by Watchman Nee
Overrun by Demons, by Thomas Ice and Robert Dean.

I don't intend to cover the same ground as these books, because it is not my intention to reinvent the wheel. There's a lot of good material on this subject. But, I would like to end this study of spiritual warfare with an example of the true practice of warfare, biblical spiritual warfare, taken from the life of Paul.

8

A Case History of True Warfare

The problem for modern believers is that this biblical model doesn't demonstrate "new revelation" or give a "novel approach". There were no immediate, spectacular results. It even involves a little rejection by man. For this reason, an increasing number of people judge this episode a failure in Paul's life, based on its results. This is a fatal mistake. I am referring to the story in Acts 17 of Paul on Mars Hill. This sermon is the exact antidote for our society of today.

A Case Study of Spiritual Warfare

Acts 17:16-21 Now while Paul waited for them at Athens, his spirit was stirred in him, when he saw the city wholly given to idolatry. Therefore disputed he in the synagogue with the Jews, and with the devout persons, and in the market daily with them that met with him. Then certain philosophers of the Epicureans and of the Stoics, encountered him. And some said, What will this babbler say? other some, He seemeth to be a setter forth of strange gods; because he preached unto them Jesus and resurrection. And they took him, and brought him unto Areopagus, saying, May we know what this new doctrine, whereof thou speakest, is? For thou bringest certain strange things to our ears; we would know therefore what these things mean. (For all the Athenians and strangers which were there spent their time in nothing else, but either to tell, or to hear some new thing.)

Here we have classic spiritual warfare! Paul, grieved by the idolatry, didn't start praying against Zeus, Apollo, or Aphrodite! He went out into the street to refute the teaching of Zeus and Apollo, in the minds of men. Look at the text. Paul is preaching, reasoning, debating, in the synagogue and marketplace. He is bringing down the demonic strongholds of thinking, and refuting the vain imaginations, cross-examining the high thinking that dares exalt itself against the knowledge of Christ. I know, some of you would rather have "warfare worship and praise marches" against Zeus or some other demon. It feels like you're getting things done! But Paul knew nothing about such things.

The Acts specifically tells us the two main philosophies represented in the crowd Paul addressed on Mars Hill. Why? Because God wants us to realize that demons usually don't hold men directly, they control men through philosophies.

***Colossians 2:8** Beware lest any man spoil you through philosophy and vain deceit, after the tradition of men, after the rudiments of the world, and not after Christ.*

Attacking the spirit of something in a direct way is really a lost cause. Demons will always be here until "the time appointed". But if we attack the philosophy in the mind of the captive, then the spirit loses his means of control. Demons control men by influencing their thinking, so this should also be the area of our counter-attack.

Who were the Epicureans and Stoics? Epicurus was a Greek philosopher who would fit very well in the talk show circuit or as a high school or college professor today. His system of ethics was thus: Good is basically whatever gives you pleasure without hurting others. The whole purpose of life is to seek your own happiness. Sound familiar? To an Epicurean, the god or gods created the world but have no interest in it. Everything is governed by chance. Living is for today, there is no afterlife. There is nothing to dread or hope for in the future. The Stoics, on the other hand, were followers of Zeno, a Greek philosopher who taught that the whole universe is governed by a blind, impersonal force called Reason, or the World Soul. This force is contained within creation, so all is God.

According to Zeno, the best way to live is to accept the circumstances that the fates have ordained. "Keep a stiff upper lip." Don't be overjoyed when good things happen, and don't get upset when bad things happen to you. In fact, Stoics didn't like emotion. They believed you are to be guided by Reason, not emotion. Stoicism believed in a cold, hard world, ruled by fate. Both Epicureanism and Stoicism believed in a remote, impersonal God who didn't care. Enter Paul, waging spiritual warfare on Mars Hill. He didn't address the strongman, the spirit of Greek philosophy. But, he took the time specifically to refute the philosophy point by point!

Point #1, Acts 17:22-23

Then Paul stood in the midst of Mars hill and said, Ye men of Athens, I perceive that in all things ye are too superstitious. For as I passed by, and beheld your devotions, I found an altar with this inscription, TO THE UNKNOWN GOD, Whom therefore ye ignorantly worship, him declare I unto you.

Paul starts off by offering this premise: you can know God because He is a personal being. Note also that first of all, Paul "relates" to his audience. "I see that you also are spiritual (religious). The God whom you call Unknown (remote, indifferent, unknowable), I'd like to introduce to you." Paganism in our day presents "God as a force", an impersonal God or a set of impartial spiritual laws. The infinite, transcendent and yet personal God of the Bible needs to be proclaimed to this generation again. God delights to be known and has revealed Himself through Jesus!

Point #2 Acts 17:24

God that made the world and all things therein, seeing that he is Lord of heaven and earth, dwelleth not in temples made with hands.

God created everything. God is not a creation, nor is creation a part of Him. One of the consequences of the Evolution myth is a tremendous confusion as to the distinction between creation and Creator. God made all things and needs nothing. All things depend on Him for their existence. God cannot be contained in a man-made temple. Nothing can contain God. When people blur the distinction between creation and Creator, idolatry flourishes and the people suffer.

Point #3 Acts 17:25

Neither is worshipped with men's hands, as though he needed any thing, seeing he giveth to all life, and breath, and all things.

God doesn't depend on us for existence. But, we need Him for every breath we take! Our culture needs this truth again. Our modern concept of God is too small. He needs us. We have to prop him up, defend him in court, send him money or he'll go off the air! If we don't join him in his fight with the devil, he will lose! Obviously, this isn't the God of the Bible. Western culture, including the Charismatic Movement, has made God in their image. The Living God doesn't depend on us, but we need him. He is the center around which we revolve, rather than our needs being His pivot of attention. We were made for His pleasure, not vice versa.

Point #4 Acts 17:26

And hath made of one blood all nations of men for to dwell on all the face of the earth, and hath determined the times before appointed, and the bounds of their habitation.

God made all men from one man, Adam. There are no levels of society, or superior races, nor are some races naturally more primitive, all that is an evolutionary concept. Literally, we all came from one blood. God created us with purpose, to fill the earth. Thus, God does not believe in birth control. Zero population growth is an affront to a holy God!

Point #5

God, who is intimately involved with the human race, set the boundaries of time and space that each person and nation should inhabit! God divided the nations. But now there is a rebellion against what God did at Babel, an ungodly desire to unite the nations of this world without Christ. Even the attempt to unite under the banner of religion is of Satan. There is no limit to the evil that fallen man can accomplish when he is in "unity". On the other hand, in Christ there is already a unity of the Spirit that cannot be manufactured. And yet God made the boundaries. God divided us. People rebel against that, they don't like boundaries. They hate borders. In the world, there is an internationalism (globalism) coming that is making people believe the day of separate nations is over. However, God made those boundaries so that people could seek Him. When there are no boundaries, people join forces until there is no limit to what they can do in their opposition to God and His cause, as exemplified at Babel.

In the Church world, there is a parallel. People want to unite regardless of doctrine, though the Word of God is the plumb line of unity. The idea now is that all peoples will unite globally in a new international Christian super-church. Millions will flock, they say, into the Church of God. If they do, they will be nominal Christians, looking for easy believism. Jesus said becoming a Christian was more than adopting a cosy religious outlook and going to a church.

Point #6 Acts 17:27-28

That they should seek the Lord, if haply they might feel after him, and find him, though he be not far from every one of us; For in him we live, and move, and have our being; as certain also of your own poets have said, For we are also his offspring.

God is not remote. He is quite immanent, desiring that men might seek Him. The idea of a remote, indifferent God who can't be known, is a Satanic deception. Like Paul, we should be waging war against this idea with Truth!

Point #7 Acts 17:29-30

Forasmuch then as we are the offspring of God, we ought not to think that the Godhead is like unto gold, or silver, or stone, graven by art and man's device. And the times of this ignorance God winked at; but now commandeth all men every where to repent.

Idolatry has things backwards. We don't make God in our image, He made us in His image! No wonder men want to "make" a god. The one who creates is the one who owns and controls.

Point #8 Acts 17:30-31

And the times of this ignorance God winked at; but now commandeth all men every where to repent; Because he hath appointed a day, in the which he will judge the world in righteousness by that man whom he hath ordained; whereof he hath given assurance unto all men, in that he hath raised him from the dead.

There is coming a day of judgment. What you do in this life is of significance. There are eternal consequences for good or evil, in what every man does and in the choices he makes. There is a life after this life. This gives meaning to human life. Man is not insignificant, and life is not pointless. History is linear – heading for a day.

Point #9 Acts 17:31-34

Because he hath appointed a day, in the which he will judge the world in righteousness by that man whom he hath ordained; whereof he hath given assurance unto all men, in that he hath raised him from the dead. And when they heard of the resurrection of the dead, some mocked; and others said, We will hear thee again of this matter. So Paul departed from among them. Howbeit certain men clave unto him, and believed; among the which was Dionysius the Areopagite and a woman named Damaris, and others with them.

There is a standard of judgment, a man God has set in the earth, the Lord Jesus. He is the standard of what God intended humanity to be. God declared Him to be the Son of God by raising him from the dead. He is all God and all man, God in the flesh, Jesus Christ!

After Paul had set forth these truths in opposition to Satan's lies, some believed and some didn't. One pitfall that we must all avoid is to judge the effectiveness of the warfare by the results. By some standards, Paul didn't seem to be too successful. The city of Athens was hardly shaken with revival. No idols crumbled. Outwardly all was calm. Such is the kingdom of God, planted as an insignificant seed, but gradually blossoming as the largest of all herbs. However, a lot of discontent is being generated by a sort of pragmatism. If it doesn't bring massive, spectacular results, we must not be doing it right. But, we don't select a preaching technique just on the basis of "it works". We do what we do because of faithfulness to God. I preach truth because it is truth, not because "it works". We have to preach the Truth, even if few respond.

People are being disillusioned by a spurious view of what we are to expect in the last days. In contrast to prophecies that tell us of "nations trembling", and millions bowing the knee to Christ, Jesus told us that the world would never embrace us, in fact, that all nations will hate us. At best, we will "call out" of this world a multitude, but not the majority. The way of eternal life is narrow and "few" there be who find it. (Spiritual warfare is all about bringing down the strongholds that prevent people from coming to Christ in the millions – it is about global revival!)

Conclusion

Today's spiritual warfare is all about man, not God. It is man's attempt to elevate himself to the "God-level" and to intervene in the plans of history. It is motivated by man's arrogance and pride – his love of this earth and this present life, and the desire to create an ideal world. But that is not of God.

I Jn 2:16-17 For all that is in the world, the lust of the flesh, and the lust of the eyes, and the pride of life, is not of the Father, but is of the world. And the world passeth away, and the lust thereof: but he that doeth the will of God abideth for ever.

Christians have forgotten, in their zeal to convert the world, that God is sovereign, and God's plan is being worked out, despite mankind!

And as for Satan, he is mocking all these human attempts to "pull down the strongholds". He knows full well that his finest hour is yet to come; that he and his cohorts will not be cast down until the appointed time. Meanwhile, he is having a pretty good game seducing unwary Christians into spiritual warfare prayer meetings, where they focus on naming spirits of evil instead of their own need for repentance before God.

Satan waves his red rag, and obediently the Christian Church charges! By all modern standards, Paul failed at spiritual warfare. He never researched the territorial spirits; he didn't rebuke the strongholds of pagan religion; he didn't see whole cities come to the Lord. Yet, in truth Paul didn't fail at spiritual warfare, he won! Paul never forgot his original commission, and did not move out of his God-given measure of influence and responsibility.

Acts 26:15-18 *And I said, Who art thou, Lord? And he said, I am Jesus whom thou persecutest. But rise, and stand upon thy feet; for I have appeared unto thee for this purpose, to make thee a minister and a witness both of these things which thou hast seen, and of those things in the which I will appear unto thee; Delivering thee from the people, and from the Gentiles, unto whom now I send thee. To open their eyes, and to turn them from darkness to light, and from the power of Satan unto God, that they may receive forgiveness of sins, and inheritance among them which are sanctified by faith that is in me.*

This was Paul's commission, and it is ours. We are called to preach the gospel of grace and forgiveness, turning men from the darkness of this world's vain philosophies to the light of truth. We can never hope to achieve that aim by attacking territorial spirits, but only by opening our mouths and witnessing of Jesus, and telling men and women the gospel truths.

We wage war against Satan most effectively when we allow God's anointed Word to go forth to touch unbelievers' hearts and souls, convicting them, converting them, and opening them up to God.

As for today's unbiblical spiritual warfare – I have one closing comment – the grace of Christ is sufficient for us, His power will be made perfect in our weakness.

Appendix One

Rodney Howard Browne: An Analysis of the Laughing Revival

He calls himself a "Holy Ghost Bartender", serving up the new wine! His services are characterized by uproarious laughter. In a typical service, Rodney Howard Browne will call people out of the crowd, point a finger at them and "send them to the floor", convulsed in laughter.[1]

Browne is a thirty three year old evangelist from South Africa. He was born and raised in a Pentecostal family, in an atmosphere that he describes as "bathed in prayer". Here is Rodney's own description of his transforming experience in July of 1979 at the age of 18.

> I knew that there was more, much more. During the years that would follow, I began to get hungry for God. In July of 1979, I cried out to God in sheer desperation. I wanted Him to manifest Himself to me and in me. I was hungry.
>
> He told me that I had to hunger and thirst. At first I said to him, 'Why don't you just give it to me? I have served you all my life. I have been a good boy. I haven't done this, I haven't done that as others have. God I deserve it.' He said, 'I'm not a respecter of persons. You come the same way everyone else does. You come in faith and you get hungry and you desire it. Then I'll give it to you.
>
> 'You have to desire it like a man who has been in the desert three days desires water. All he can cry for is water. If a man walks up to him and offers him half a million dollars, he will push him aside and shout, no, water, water, water! He wants water more than life itself, because the only thing that is going to save him is water.'
>
> When you become desperate for the Holy Ghost in your life like that, so that you want nothing else, then He will come. There is

something about a hungry and thirsty heart that will cause God's power to move over a million people and come to your house.

As I prayed that day, I told the Lord, 'Either you come down here and touch me, or I am going to come up there and touch you.' I was desperate. I must have called out to God for about twenty minutes that day.

Suddenly the fire of God fell on me. It started on my head and went right down to my feet. His power burned in my body and stayed like that for three whole days. I thought I was going to die. I thought, 'He has heard my prayer, 'Either you come down and touch me or I will come up and touch you', and now He has come down here and touched me and He is going to kill me and take me home.'

I was really praying, 'Lord I'm too young to die.' In the fourth day, I am not praying, 'O Lord, send your glory, I'm praying, please lift it off me so that I can bear it.' I was plugged into heaven's electric light supply and since then my desire has been to go and plug other people in.

My whole body was on fire from the top of my head to the soles of my feet. Out of my belly began to flow a river of living water. I began to laugh uncontrollably and then I began to weep and then speak with other tongues.

I was so intoxicated on the wine of the Holy Ghost that I was literally beside myself. The fire of God was coursing through my whole being and it didn't quit...He did finally lift that intense anointing off me, but it stayed lightly on me, that I was aware of, for two weeks. Because of that encounter with the Lord, my life was radically changed from that day on.[2]

Rodney went on to become an associate pastor at South Africa's RHEMA church in Johannesburg, for two years. In December 1987 Browne arrived in Orlando, Florida to begin an evangelistic ministry here in the States.

In April of 1989, Browne's travelling ministry had him in Albany, New York, when an unusual manifestation occurred. As He was preaching, he and others in the service felt a "sensation like a heavy blanket coming over him...". People began falling out of their seats, some were laughing and others were crying. The noise got so loud that Browne had to interrupt his sermon. "Lord, you're ruining my meeting", the evangelist complained. He says God replied, "The way your meetings have been going lately, they deserve to be ruined. I will move all the time if you will allow me to move."[3]

From that time on, Browne increased in demand as a speaker. The greatest turning point occurred in the Spring of 1993. Browne held a four week meeting in Lakeland, Florida at Carpenter's Home Church. The 10,000 seat auditorium was filled almost every night. People were reported to have been drawn from as far away as Africa, Great Britain, and Argentina. What were they drawn to? The unusual phenomena of laughter. As **Charisma Magazine** reports,

> No matter what Howard Browne did or said, hundreds who attended the daily sessions always ended up on the sanctuary floor in helpless laughter. When the services were broadcast on the radio, more curious seekers showed up to join the fun.[4]

Curious? Fun? The article goes on to report that the church added 800 new members, and its income went up 30%! They baptized 2,200, according to the Pastor, Karl Strader.

At the risk of being perceived as critical, please allow me to raise some objections. Be a Berean, think this stuff over, long and hard. Pray much and search the scriptures. I might be off, Rodney Howard Browne might be off, or he might be God's gift. I just want to raise some issues to provoke critical thinking. We do have the treasure in earthen vessels. As one professor said, "It's the dirt and divinity principle." Which means that in every revival or move of God, there is going to be both the human element and the divine, as well as the opposition of the demonic. Far be it from me to sit in final judgement on this ministry as though I were God, but on the other hand, any thing truly born of God can endure the scrutiny of the Berean treatment. There are just a few issues I shall raise for your evaluation.

The Issue of Sensuality

II Peter 2:2 And many shall follow their pernicious (lit. sensual) *ways: by reason of whom the way of truth shall be evil spoken of.*
Jude 19 These be they who separate themselves, sensual, having not the Spirit.

The word sensual does not always refer to sexuality. It is more of a reference to the things pertaining to the senses. Both Jude and Peter warn us of the sensual nature of false prophets and apostles. We have a sensual culture. Consequently, truth is not enough, people have to feel God. The preaching of the cross, or of Christ is fine and dandy, but we want to see whole sections of the crowd fall under the power, feel the heavy blanket of anointing, see the glory cloud. The music has to be just right, before the Spirit comes. Can you see that sensuality has saturated the preaching of Christ? The ministers who draw the masses, all too often are the ones who can create an atmosphere, almost a Pentecostal version of a Catholic mass! Remember the mass? It wasn't the sermon that was important, it was the atmosphere. The incense, robes, candles, songs, and the wafer. You felt the atmosphere, the content of the sermon didn't really matter. Any more, in Pentecostal circles, the content of sermons is almost irrelevant, (who needs doctrine?). The atmosphere is all essential. "Do you feel the presence tonight?", a minister will ask. We no longer worship God just because He is, we keep on singing and worshipping until we "come into that feeling". "Wow, God was really in that service!", someone says. You mean God isn't in all of them? That one service where all you did was pray, or where the pastor preached good doctrine, but you felt nothing, was probably the most important service you ever attended!

There is a heightened sensuality that has been cultivated. A lot can happen in that kind of atmosphere. Even in Rodney Howard Browne's testimony the emphasis seemed to be more on feelings than truth. The idea is that it was a radical, life-changing experience with God, that changed him. Hearing that testimony will develop a hunger all right, but a hunger for what? The feeling of fire or electricity coursing through my being? If I only get that, will I be all right?

Let me quote Rodney about an early ministry experience:

> **It is one thing to be anointed of God. It is another thing to be in a position to release that anointing to others, seeing their lives touched**

with the reality of that *heavenly materiality*. [emphasis mine].
I can remember the day it first happened – the day my life and ministry changed ... We were preaching in a Methodist church. I was back in the vestibule – which is a holy name for a plain old office – preparing for the service. One of the young ladies came into the office and asked me to pray for her because she was in terrible pain. I stood up from the chair where I was sitting and lifted my right hand as I normally would do to lay hands on her and pray. Then the most amazing thing happened.
I got my hand halfway to her head, almost like a gunslinger would draw a gun out of his holster and point it at his opponent. Suddenly, unexpectedly, it felt like my finger tips came off. I felt a full volume of the anointing flow out of my hand. The only way I can explain it is like a fireman holding a fire hose with a full volume of water coming out of it. The anointing went right into her. It looked like someone had hit her in the head with an invisible baseball bat and she fell to the floor.[5]

Now this makes for some interesting reading, I am not saying this is unscriptural or demonic, I believe in laying on of hands, speaking in tongues, and casting out devils. But the emphasis here, seems to me, to be subtly sensual. The reader here, reads about power flowing from the hand, like a fire hose, people dropping like flies, instant healing, and if you go on in the book, a whole service of people getting drunk in the Spirit and Rodney Howard Browne amusingly trying to sober them up before the priest gets there! Wow, I want that! I want to feel the anointing flow from my hand like a fire hose! Do you see what I'm saying? In a subtle way the focus is being shifted from the compassion of Jesus for hurting people, to the "power in the hand", or amusing anecdotes of how religious authorities try to cope with Holy Ghost people.

In the same way, the sensuality is cultivated in a typical service. For one thing, you come to a Rodney Howard Browne service knowing that the trademark is laughter. You expect to either laugh or resist laughing. Laughing is contagious. Who doesn't want a laugh? To be called out of a crowd in a laughing service, and pointed at by a "laughing evangelist" where people are expecting you to get hit by "holy laughter" must be quite an experience. I'm even laughing right now just thinking about it, but I laugh easily. The question I have is this, did the apostles do it? Or have we got something new, for a new generation?

The idea that it is an experience, (rather than truth acted on), that transforms people is setting people up for deception. It is truth that sets you free. What truth are people responding to, that makes them laugh raucously, interrupting the word of God? In Rodney's own words:

> We were in a meeting in Pittsburgh, Penn. in January 1990 and the glory of the Lord was in the place. Most of the people were not in their seats. They were lying on the floor, under the power of God.
> The presence of God came in like a cloud and people were filled with joy. It was bubbling out of their bellies. People were totally drunk in the Holy Ghost. The anointing of God was on them and they were in a place of Holy Ghost ecstasy, total joy. They were beside themselves.

In another meeting:

> While I was preaching, the power of God began to fall. Many people began to fall out of their seats. It looked like someone was shooting them and in some places, whole rows would go down. They were laughing and crying and falling all over the place and looked like drunken people.
> I tried to preach above the noise of the people but to no avail. The glory of the Lord fell in such a wonderful way. Some were healed in their seats. The Lord then said to me, "I will move all the time if you will allow me to."[6]

If you want an experience, try the transfiguration! And yet Peter, James, and John, who witnessed Jesus, Moses, and Elijah, conversing about the cross, and heard God's voice from the cloud of glory, could not tell anybody of the experience until after the resurrection. Peter would later write that it is the "more sure word of prophecy", (scripture), that we do well to take heed to.

***II Peter 1:16-19** For we have not followed cunningly devised fables, when we made known unto you the power and coming of our Lord Jesus Christ, but were eye witnesses of his majesty. For he received from God the Father honour and glory, when there came such a voice to him from the excellent glory, This is my beloved Son, in whom I am well pleased. And this voice which came from heaven we heard, when we were with him in the holy mount. We* *have also a more sure word of prophecy; where unto ye do well that ye take heed, as unto a light that shineth in a dark place, until the day dawn, and the day star arise in your hearts.*

In his teaching, Browne even appeals to sensual confirmation:

> I was in another meeting and was walking around the church praying for several folk as I felt prompted by the Lord. When I went to pray for a dear brother sitting to the left of me, he stood up and hugged me. Then he told me that he had died several years ago, and had left his body for a time and was caught up into glory. He said he knew that what was happening was real because he had witnessed that same presence of the Holy Ghost – the glory of God – when he crossed over to the other side.[7]

That is not a good test of what is genuine or not. Jesus told us that if they don't believe Moses and the prophets then they won't believe even if someone come from the other side. You can only die once, then the judgment. Consequently, I reject all stories, "from the other side", except the true witness of the other side, the Lord Jesus Christ.

In the recent article **Charisma** magazine did on Howard Browne, Browne himself is quoted as saying,

> The proof that this is a move of God, is that when I leave, it doesn't stop. I'm just the Holy Ghost bartender. I just serve the new wine and invite them to drink.

The Issue of Reverence

This brings me to another issue of concern, the reverence issue. Holy Ghost bartender? Laughing so loud a preacher can't preach God's word? The "new wave" that seems to be coming has what I would consider to be an irreverent side to it. For example, an Episcopal rector, Hugh Williams, reports visiting the revival meetings after hearing about the laughter on the radio. I think his testimony in Charisma underscores the point I'm trying to make. This testimony, incidentally, is not antagonistic to Rodney Howard Browne, but rather, is the testimony of one who feels renewed from the meetings.

After two meetings, he was not impressed; during the third, Howard Browne called him and three others out into the aisle and simply said, 'Be filled!'. 'Boom! Down I went in the Spirit', says Williams, 'And I started laughing. I laughed so hard for twenty minutes, my throat was sore the next day. I've been Charismatic for 14 years, but I'd dried out and grown tired. This refreshed me personally and changed my marriage.' So why would God use laughter to bring spiritual renewal? Williams says many people today need more than words – they need a demonstration of God's power. 'Words have become meaningless in our society', he says, 'Signs and wonders are what must recapture our attention.'[8]

The article goes on to say that on Palm Sunday, 1993, Williams was hit by a fit of laughter – just as he was about to read from the gospels! Dressed in his priestly garments he fell to the floor, laughing, to the amazement of his parishioners. Another episode is recounted in which,

laughter broke out during the consecratory prayer for the Eucharist, normally the most solemn part of the service. 'It is distracting', Williams says, 'But I've come to feel it is God who's distracting us from our routine ways and concentrating our attention on Him'.[8]

No matter what you think of Episcopal liturgy, anyone in their right mind realizes that the Eucharist is a solemn, holy time. We are to do this in remembrance of Him. I doubt Jesus was rolling on the ground laughing as He reminded the apostles, "This is my body, this is my blood, do this in remembrance of me." As far as God wanting our attention, I always thought that the word of God, communion, and worship was the time honoured way that God had our attention. Is God throwing that out as not having worked? If anything it is the one who disrupts reverent, sacred things like preaching and communion, that is the one who wants attention.

Unbelievably, Browne testifies,

One night I was preaching on hell, and [laughter] just hit the whole place. The more I told people what hell was like, the more they laughed. When I gave an alter call, they came forward by the hundreds to be saved.

Saved? Saved from what? This testimony is proof that Charismatic Christians are actually being re-conditioned to an irrational bias. The meaning of concepts and words and doctrine is being reversed! The old way is to weep and mourn, for you have sinned against an infinitely holy and good God. The modern "revelation" is to laugh your way down to the altar, right in the face of warnings against you of God's judgement. The delusion spoken of in II Thessalonians 2 is here. This is the lie that thousands and millions will believe, because they have never received a love for the truth.

I think that the ultimate warning flag is Browne's endorsement by Oral and Richard Roberts. According to **Charisma**,

> **[Richard] Roberts says he ended up on the floor laughing at every Howard Browne meeting, as have members of his family. His father, Oral Roberts, eventually proclaimed that Howard Browne's ministry signalled the arrival of another level in the Holy Spirit.**

Then **Charisma** insightfully adds,

> **No one doubts that having vast numbers of listeners convulsed in laughter can make whatever is being said from the pulpit irrelevant.**

Evidently Oral could hardly prophesy over Browne, because of the volume of the laughter in the auditorium.[9]

The Bias Against Truth

The third concern is that it is fostering a bias against truth, or I should say it is exposing a pre-existing anti-truth bias. As I said earlier the idea is that it is the experience that will make you free. In fact, the idea is subtly being propagated that it is the irrational experience, that sets you free! After all, what possible rationale could there be, in laughing uproariously about hell? Jesus' signs and wonders may have exceeded reason, but they didn't contradict it. Jesus preached much on hell, if anyone did laugh at it, Jesus had a simple response, "Woe to those who laugh now, you shall weep!"

It is a subtle rebellion that secretly says, "We'll fly in the face of what the 'conventional' church stands for. We are more in tune, more Spirit-filled. **They** preach with conviction, **we** laugh!"

Rodney Howard Browne is one of those preachers who is so loving to everybody except those who would dare criticize. Here are some quotes from his book, "Since when does God give the right to an individual to be the watch dog of the church and to bite and devour one another for the protection of the gospel", and "I pray the church would have as much sense as the pharisee Gamaliel and stop criticizing, thinking God set them as the watch dog of the church...". Also, "It is important to realize that criticism is the anointing (clothing) of the flesh. It needs to pull others down in order to lift itself up."[10]

Why criticize critics? Maybe they aren't fighting God, maybe they are Bereans. Any move of God that is genuine, doesn't need to rail against the critics, just let God vindicate you! Now if the critics are trying to examine you by a human standard, that's wrong, but could there be anything wrong with holding up a ministry to examination in the light of the word?

The conditioning against truth and discernment has taken a step up lately, into a higher dimension. Between Paul and Jan Crouch railing about heresy hunters, and evangelists like Rodney Howard Browne, scorning the "religious dead heads", who quench the Spirit, there is almost a hatred, at least a spirit of mockery, "The religious crowd who don't go along with the flow are just hilarious, we who are spiritual scorn them."

It all goes along with the anti-doctrine bias, prevalent in the world today. This bias supports the idea that doctrine is irrelevant, it is for the stuffy, the ones who just want "head knowledge". If we would just yield, surrender to the Spirit, just turn off our minds, then the Spirit would have his way. A whole generation has been raised up with these anti-thought biases, they have been conditioned to go along with many irrational things, without raising any objections.

This stems from a fundamental misunderstanding about Christianity. Christianity is not anti-intellectual!

***Proverbs 19:2** Also, that the soul be without knowledge is not good; and he that hasteth with his feet sinneth.*

It may be simple faith, I agree, simple in the sense of sincere and uncomplicated, but that doesn't mean simplistic, naive, and gullible. A strong Christian is an informed Christian. As John says, the Son of God has come and given us an understanding. (I John 5:20) You shall know the truth and the truth shall make you free. You never see Jesus or the apostles telling anyone to "Turn off your head and go with the experience." Christianity is supernatural indeed. I speak in tongues, cast out devils, and have seen many healings. I have even been caught up in the Spirit and laughed myself whole! But I've never been "led" to laugh at communion, or in a sermon on hell, or while any preacher is preaching God's word. This is irrational and shouldn't be trusted.

I would like to ask any of these people who testified, what truth did you conform to? Which truth transformed your life? I don't believe that God transforms without truth and I am very leery of this concept. It is the devil who offers the transforming experience not based on truth. The Guru touches the sceptic and he devotes his life to him or the hypnotist alters the conscience and creates the spectacle for everyone's amusement. These are transforming experiences without the basis of truth. But God addresses the mind, appeals to the conscience, the gospel truly makes good sense! Even Paul's conversion experience, was not void of truth. He had actually been under conviction for quite some time, having heard Stephan's sermon and seen truth lived in the way he died. It is the truth that transforms, not the unusual, bizarre experience. A young friend of mine went to Rodney Howard Browne for a "change in his life". He was living with his girlfriend outside of marriage, and they both went to the meeting. They both entered into the laughter, and really "felt the Spirit". They were ministered to that way. Did they repent? No, why should they? They were touched just the way they were. I hope you can see that all that God is saying to this adulterous generation is being swept aside as irrelevant, but boy did we ever have church! Wow, I felt it!

Repentance

The above testimony brings me to my next concern. The desperate need is for repentance. An interesting story comes from the revival at Azusa street at the turn of the century. It seems that Frank Bartleman was in one of the services and during the singing of worship songs, he was led to make them stop. "Quit worshipping, you are singing away your conviction of sin." Even good things can become a hindrance when used out of context. This is what I'm afraid this laughing revival is doing, laughing away repentance. James had a strong word to say about this.

***James 4:9-10** Be afflicted, and mourn, and weep; let your laughter be turned to mourning, and your joy to heaviness. Humble yourselves in the sight of the Lord, and he shall lift you up. In biblical thought, laughing is usually associated with derision and scorn. Not always, mind you, Jesus and the apostles laughed, but not uncontrollably. The Christian is being confused on this very issue today. The way out of the confusion is to realize that there is a huge difference between laughter and joy.*

***Proverbs 14:13** Even in laughter the heart is sorrowful; and the end of that mirth is heaviness.*

To call this laughing revival an "outburst of Christian joy", to me is to misunderstand joy. Just because you were invited to laugh at the meeting doesn't mean you have joy in your life, nor is it God's way of cultivating joy. If anything, joy comes out of us in the midst of suffering various trials, always because of what we believe.

***Romans 15:13** Now the God of hope fill you with all joy and peace in believing, that ye may abound in hope, through the power of the Holy Ghost.*
***II Corinthians 8:2** How that in a great trial of affliction the abundance of their joy and their deep poverty abounded unto the riches of their liberality.*

I Thessalonians 1:6 *And ye became followers of us, and of the Lord, having received the word in much affliction, with joy of the Holy Ghost.*

In many cases, the joy that followers of Browne's meetings are bringing back to their churches, isn't the fruit of the Spirit. Reports are already circulating about "laugh inciters" breaking up sermons. People unable to quit laughing, laughing at inappropriate times and occasions. This is more of a forced, contrived laughter, which draws attention to the laughter, not the Lord.

I can experience the joy of the Holy Ghost, without laughing. The joy of the Spirit goes deeper than "funny" or irrational. It doesn't come from meetings, laying on of hands or contagious laughter. It comes from that deep abiding faith that no matter what comes, He will never leave me or forsake me. God gives it to those who "love righteousness and hate iniquity". (Hebrews 1:8) It is a result of being born again to a living hope, not being pointed at in some giddy meeting.

We all want a move of the Spirit, we long for revival. I don't doubt for one minute that Rodney Howard Browne and his wife want to bring revival to America, but sincerity is no guarantee that someone is "right on". You'll know them by their fruits. Are people being turned to the Lord or to self? Is Jesus the emphasis or is it experience? If Jesus is the focal point, why didn't he ever promote this experience? Would the apostles have done this? What is the content of Rodney's message? What is he actually saying?

It is my prayer that this writing will allow you to this in a firm but loving spirit. Rodney Howard Browne and his followers most likely want heaven sent revival. So do we. Pray for them as well as inform yourself and others.

Beware

1. Beware the non-apostolic experience I agree Christianity is supernatural and has an awe inspiring aspect to it. But not all supernaturalism is holy. A good guide is the apostles. Did they

practice this? If not, why do we believe we should? Is there new truth?

2. Beware the feeling of your own sincerity. So few believe Jeremiah 17:9. Our heart has a way of baptizing our wrong desires, telling us they are "of God". On top of that false prophets appeal to those same desires assuring us of fame, success, and esteem. Thinking you are sincere is no safeguard against seduction, it sets you up for it.

3. Beware of mental passivity and appeals to shut off your mind and go with the Spirit, they are misguided, at best, and possibly Satanic. Jesus and the apostles never called upon people to shut off their minds! God calls us to love Him with all of our faculties, including our minds. Therefore beware of any denigrating of the word of doctrine.

Think about it!

Appendix One References

1. Julia Duin. **Charisma** Magazine "Praise the Lord and Pass the New Wine." On Rodney Howard Browne. August 1994.
2. Rodney Howard Browne. **The Touch of God**. RHBEA Publications. Page 73-74.
3. Charisma Article. Page 23
4. Ibid. Page 24.
5. Howard Browne. Pages 75-76.
6. Ibid. Pages 99-100.
7. Ibid. Page 101.
8. Charisma Article.
9. Charisma Article.

10. Howard Browne. Page vii. From Introduction.

Appendix Two

Spiritual Warfare – Quo Vadis?*

Reprinted From "Mainstream" Spring 1994
Banner Ministries, UK

The city of La Planta, Argentina, June 1992. A year of spiritual mapping has taken place to identify the six spirits that control the city. In a four hour prayer meeting, the Christians of La Planta confess the sins of its inhabitants and ask God "to erase the consequences of sin". Now the time has come – a small group of leaders work in pairs, one to break the power of each ruling spirit and one to call forth "the opposite spirit" in exchange.[1]

What is going on here? This is modern spiritual warfare! Gone is the simple biblical concept of withstanding the devices of the devil in our personal Christian walk. Now huge sections of the Church are involved in "taking cities for God" by intensive historical research, warfare prayer and the remission of corporate sin.

There is much confusion over spiritual warfare today. Those who support its use as an evangelistic tool, often fail to grasp the deeper implications. They are looking at isolated problems and isolated results. They miss the wood for the trees! The few who do stand back and view the spiritual warfare scene as a whole are sounding the alarm. Here's why:

> **Today's praying church is rising up in militant force to possess the promised land of our nations.**[2]

> **There is no reason why we, the Church, should concede one square inch of this planet to the government of territorial spirits. This is our planet.**[3]

> **All spiritual warfare is waged over one essential question: who will**

control reality on earth – heaven or hell?... We must see that our prayers, attitudes and agreement with God are an integral part of establishing the reality of the kingdom of God on earth![4]

The ultimate aim in spiritual warfare is to take this world – its physical land, its people, and all created things – cause it to submit to God, then rule and reign over it as God's Chosen People.

Replacement Theology

> We begin to take dominion in spiritual areas by casting out devils and discerning spirits... finally, we begin to rule and reign with Christ. We rule and reign in social settings, in the heavenlies, and here on earth.[5]

Leaders today recognize that no worldwide godly kingdom can exist while Satan and his fallen angels hold sway in the heavenlies. They believe these powers must be replaced if there is to be any change in world government – and they are right! For it IS God's ultimate intention to cast down fallen angels, and to rule the world Himself, with the co-operation of His people. Yet it is not the Church's role to effect this victory.

Roger Forster, one of the four founders of the March For Jesus, disagrees. In his foreword to the book Territorial Spirits, he writes:

> Heb 2:5 reveals to us that the world to come will no longer be under subjection to angels but will be under subjection to redeemed men and women who will reign with Christ. We are at present in training for reigning.[6]

But the "world to come" spoken of in that Hebrews passage is not the present age ruled by a triumphant Church. It is the Millennial age ruled by the Lord Jesus as King and Messiah. Forster continues:

> These structures [territorial principalities] will be *refurbished with a whole new personnel.* The final overthrow of Satan's rebellious colonial government by the central government of God is preceded by the faith-sons of Abraham bringing blessing to all the families of

earth. This demands *territorial claims* and advance through the earth."[7] [emphasis added]

So here we have a new form of "replacement theology"! The Church replaces the territorial spirits and governs the nations of the world. Forster even believes that the coming of the Lord Jesus is delayed until enough people can be trained up for this role. God, he says, is allowing fallen angels to remain in place only to maintain order in the universe, and to give time for the training of a resistance movement on earth.

Eventually, this resistance movement can produce sufficient numbers of trained personnel to take over the authority and administration of the colony from Satan and his angels, giving the least amount of disturbance to the heavenly structural powers... until such a network of resistance against Satan is found all over the earth, the second coming of our Lord is held up and his total reign restrained...[8]

In God's timing, and by His command, men and women who are united with Christ will rule and reign with their Lord. Believers will share the glory of the reign of Christ – that is their promised inheritance – yet it is conditional upon their submission to His will here and now. There is no earthly government that can be set up by the Church, in this present age, that would not contravene scripture.

The coming of this world's king and the establishment of the earthly kingdom are events that come about through a sovereign act of the Lord God, not by the Church's spiritual warfare campaign. It is God who has ordained the nations, boundaries, and authorities of this world, (Acts 17:26) and only He has the authority and wisdom to rearrange them.

The timing is also important. The Bible does not teach that the Church will cast Satan and his fallen powers out of the heavenlies. On the contrary, that battle takes place only when believers have been removed from earth! Furthermore, it happens as a result of that event:

***Rev. 12:7-9** War broke out in heaven; Michael and his angels fought against the dragon, and the dragon and his angels fought,* *but they did not prevail, nor was a place found for them in heaven any longer, so the dragon was cast out – he was cast to the earth, and his angels were cast out with him.*

Only then does the victory cry go up –

NOW salvation and strength and the kingdom of our God and the power of His Christ have come, for the accuser of our brethren...has been cast down. (Rev 12:10)

And what is the result of this downfall of the heavenly spiritual hierarchy? Spiritual warfare proponents talk of pulling down spiritual strongholds and defeating Satan in order to replace his evil empire with a Christian government. They believe their activities will bring about worldwide revival, and lead to a new era of righteousness and peace. How mistaken they are! The Bible tells us that the worst is yet to come! After Satan and his fallen angels are cast out of the heavenlies, they set up a global antichrist kingdom and let loose a reign of terror! Instead of the promised universal godliness, we have universal rebellion. Instead of the millions "bowing the knee to Jesus" as many spiritual warfare teachers claim, we see in scripture that all the world worships the Beast – the antichrist!

Woe to the inhabiters of the earth and of the sea! for the devil is come down unto you, having great wrath, because he knoweth that he hath but a short time. (Rev 12:12)

The prospect of dislodging and replacing heavenly rulers appears in several handbooks on spiritual warfare, none the less. This is done by releasing the "redemptive gifts" of a city or area. (Omaha, Nebraska, for example, was once the supply station for wagon trains taking pioneers westwards. This means it can become an equipment center for spiritual pioneers!!)

Our cities contain what I call a redemptive gift...a city develops a creaturehood or personality...I believe God has participated in the creation of our cities both in forming their personality and in stationing high-ranking guardian angels over each one.[9]

Authors are wary about identifying these "redemptive gifts" as good spirits, but in the description of La Planta's battle that begins this article, the idea is clearly there. Spiritual warfare teacher John Dawson says that,

> Determining your city's redemptive gift is even more important than discerning the nature of its evil principalities.[10]

This is because casting down the stronghold is not enough to produce a change. A replacement for the stronghold must be found. After defeating and binding the territorial spirits over a city, the vacuum must be filled, says another author:

> Speak restoration of the city to its original calling. Each city has been established by God for His purpose, even if it looks as if the enemy has taken it over. [The] redemptive gift [of Resistencia, Argentina] was...the arts and music. God wanted these used in various ways for His Kingdom... We released those gifts to do their good work.[11]

Presumptuous?

Convinced of their mission to save the world, men and women confidently go about rearranging the spiritual leadership of the nations! By pronouncing a binding on evil and "releasing" goodness, they hope to transform cities into models of righteousness! But what do they actually accomplish?

I believe it is foolish and dangerous to use the Name of Jesus, and strong commanding prayers, in areas that are hidden to the Church on earth. (Deut 29:29)

These spiritual warfare activists are playing with fire! In their arrogance, they rebuke high-ranking spiritual powers, without understanding what will result!

Presumptuous are they, self-willed, they are not afraid to speak evil of dignities. Whereas angels, which are greater in power and might, bring not railing accusation against them before the Lord. **(2 Peter 2:10-11)**

What are dignities? They are angelic powers – principalities. Peter says that to rebuke and rail at these powers is something even God's angels shrink from doing. But today's presumptuous leaders think nothing of commanding and rebuking such powers.

The Deceptive Counterfeit

It should be obvious to Bible students that "releasing good spirits" over a city will not produce Christians. It might (at best) produce a hunger for a better way of life, but good works was never the path to the true Kingdom of God. Indeed, it was seeking a righteousness outside of Christ that caused Israel to fall. (Rom 10:3)

On the other hand, there is a serpentine subtlety in what is happening in the world and Church right now. People are being attracted to the idea of the antichrist kingdom because it is being presented as **a counterfeit Millennium** – it is offered as a path to peace, harmony and "goodness". So pulling down territorial spirits that cause mayhem on earth (if they do – and this has never been conclusively proved) and replacing them with "good" spirits is a flawed idea from the start. It could only produce a counterfeit of righteousness that has nothing to do with Jesus Christ, but one that artificially fulfils mankind's yearning for peace and safety.

Nevertheless, just such a "revival" has been pushed for decades, and now there are signs that it's really happening. People's spiritual hunger, brought about by years of moral and social decay, is now being filled by powerful supernatural experiences that have nothing to do with true revival. The counterfeit is here! It seems so good, it feels so real, it has the backing of the Church leadership – so how can it be wrong? What most Christians fail to see is that much of the Church leadership has sold out to a new world view that puts world revival in place of the Tribulation and preaches a glorious new

Christian Empire in place of the Second Coming of Christ.

To set up a counterfeit kingdom with a counterfeit christ in order to ensnare all mankind – this is Satan's ultimate goal. The Church's declared aim in spiritual warfare teaching is to win the world for Christ. The two aims seem totally incompatible – but are they? Are Christians being duped, and led into a situation where they actually help to fulfil the Satanic master plan? If Christians continue to ignore all warnings, to toss doctrine out of the window, to sneer at correction, to follow subjective revelations, and to dance to the dictates of their human passions – how can they avoid doing Satan's dirty work for him and end by accomplishing the very thing they plan to avoid? Believers, pray that those who have an ear to hear will listen to the Holy Spirit before it is too late!

Appendix Two References

* Quo Vadis? "Whither Goest Thou?" Famous Latin quotation taken from Jn 13:36.
1. Wagner, C.P. **Breaking Strongholds In Your City**. 1993. Pages 190-192.
2. Jacobs, Cindy. **Possessing The Gates Of The Enemy**. Marshall Pickering 1991. Page 15.
3. Dawson, John. **Taking Our Cities For God**. Word UK 1989. Page 158.
4. Frangipane, Francis. **The Three Battlegrounds**. Advancing Church Publications 1989. Page 86.
5. Paulk, Bishop Earl. **Wounded Body Of Christ**. Dimension 1983. Page 118.
6. Forster, Roger and Wagner, C.P. **Territorial Spirits**. Sovereign World. Page x.
7. Ibid.
8. Ibid.
9. Dawson. Pages 39-40.
10. Ibid.
11. Jacobs. Page 246.

Appendix Three

Spiritual Warfare And Evangelism

Reprinted From "Mainstream" Winter 1993/Spring 1994
Banner Ministries, UK

One of the key elements of spiritual warfare, and the one that draws most support for it, is evangelism. Supposedly, spiritual warfare cleans the heavens of opposition to the gospel, and opens the way for whole cities and nations to receive Christ.

Naturally, all those who love the Lord want to see others saved. So, the word "evangelism" elicits a hot-button response from Christians. Whatever else may be wrong with the Church today, "evangelism" is something we see as totally positive and good. It creates a mental picture of good old gospel preaching, tears of repentance, decisions for Christ, and new members for our church. What could possibly be wrong with such a vision? The answer is, nothing – so long as the vision is correct and tallies with the facts. But does it?

Questions

With modern evangelism, as with every area of life these days, we are forced to ask questions. The age of innocence is over. The days in which we naively trusted our elders and teachers, and carelessly endorsed their every initiative are long gone. Now, the question at the base of all our investigations is: does this square with the Word of God?

Any who are genuinely engaged in soul-winning activities deserve our support. But at the same time, we must not give blanket approval to ALL that goes by the name of evangelism, simply because it uses biblical terminology.

Few realize how deeply compromised are the organizations promoting spiritual warfare and world evangelism. As well as the new world view of Restoration, the errors of Feminism, Humanism, and Reconstructionalism, there is the Roman Catholic input. Look back far enough and you will see the guiding hand of Rome everywhere. Rome has adopted a new "evangelistic" face, while continuing to preach a false gospel. She is no friend of the truth, yet she is willing to hide her hatred of true Christianity in order to harness the energy of Protestant evangelistic organizations to achieve her own ends. There are also New Age links, incredible as that seems.

So, I make no apology for interrupting the smooth course of the ongoing world revival with my bothersome questions, praying that all Bereans will follow suit.

1. What is the true aim of today's "Evangelism"?

Healing The Land – A Quest For Kingdom Now

The natural desire of every Christian is to see souls saved, but at the same time we cannot simply close our eyes to all evangelistic outreaches trusting that they are biblically sound. Pure gospel preaching is not the only thing on the spiritual warfare agenda! Its foundational idea is that the Kingdom of God cannot come, nor can the Lord Jesus return, until all nations bow the knee to Jesus and submit to God's rule, exercised through His agency on earth, the Church.

Thus, there is an urgency to finalize the plans for restoration. The vision is for global revival and "millions of souls saved". A secular writer comments on such plans:

In the 1970s, reacting against the hesitancy of many pre-millennialists to enter the public arena, some evangelicals abandoned pre-millennialism altogether to embrace "reconstruction" or "dominion" theology, a kind of fundamentalist post-millennialism committed to achieving a Christianized world in the present age. Reconstructionalists insisted that Christians must take seriously God's command to Adam and Eve to exercise "dominion" over the earth and "subdue it". This meant, they argued, aggressive action to impose Christ's rule on the world now, BEFORE His return at Armageddon. While post-millennialists of an earlier day had focused on issues of social justice, the reconstructionalists were more preoccupied with imposing their own stern morality on the world – (their) strategy remained vague, but their long-term objective was clear:

> **Our goal is world dominion but under Christ's lordship, a world take-over if you will – we are the shapers of world history."**[1]

A much-used definition of the Kingdom in Restoration literature is: "The will and rule of God at present exercised and demonstrated through the Church". Thus, evangelism entails not only preaching the gospel of individual salvation, but also challenging national powers and governments to submit to King Jesus. Restoration leader, Roger Mitchell, writing in **The Kingdom Factor** (Marshall-Pickering, 1986) says,

> **It is unequivocally the task of evangelism ... to warn the government and its leaders of the situation they are in.**

Restoration leaders see the Kingdom in terms of taking dominion over this world and its people. They believe that the Church's given task is to alter society radically, and to bring nations into submission to the feet of Jesus. Their gospel, therefore, (as well as the conventional idea of personal conversion) is one of salvation from oppression, suffering, poverty, and distress by a return to the kingdom rule of God.

Another Restoration writer explains,

> **Jesus didn't preach the 'simple gospel' of 'only believe'. While salvation is a matter of personal response, Jesus' declared aim was that the whole world should be saved and all men be drawn to him. Often, he arrived at the need for forgiveness of sin through a confrontation of the social issues of his day...if we are to change the world, we must proclaim a gospel that tells the poor that this is the**

year of the Lord's favour, in which there is freedom for the prisoners, recovery of sight to the blind, and release for the oppressed.[2]

Today's evangelism, therefore, has at least one additional aim: the transformation of society.

Spiritual Warfare

Then there is the spiritual warfare aspect. The mistaken interpretation of certain scriptures, such as Psalm 110:1, and Acts 3:21 leads some to believe that Jesus Christ is "held" in the heavenlies until the Church finishes the job of taking dominion over this worldly scene. Some say that the Church must "subdue all God's enemies" before Christ can return. How can this be achieved, given the present world's attitude of antagonism towards the gospel? Through warfare in the heavenly realm! "The Kingdom is taken by godly Christians through fervent, commanding, binding prayer..."[3]

Much modern-day evangelism starts out from the belief that the only real obstacle to global revival is the presence in the heavenlies of evil territorial spirits. These spirit-rulers are blinding the eyes of unbelievers. If these spirits were to be overthrown – and even more so if they were to be replaced by Christians – then the nations would accept Christ's rule. So the thinking goes. Thus, conventional evangelism has to be supplemented by spiritual warfare to "enable people" to respond. Perhaps an appropriate illustration of this is the **Jesus March** – an event that many participants perceive as straight evangelism.

What is the focus of these marches? Is it simply to save souls, to preach the gospel? NO. In the book, **March For Jesus**, written by the four founders of the marches, it is explicitly denied that the aim is evangelism. The aim is to take the nations by spiritual warfare. Gerald Coates says:

> Marching for Jesus is a prophetic act which demonstrates that the meek shall inherit the earth. Each footstep on the march is an action which claims the ground and says – this is God's world and we are

> claiming it for God – our marching says that we do not inherit the world by buying it, not by inheriting but by shifting the spiritual powers that have been allocated in the nations...⁴

Roger Forster admits,

> God told us to march – our understanding of the theology of what we were doing came later.⁵

The four leaders felt they had to obey the prompts they were getting, and they worked out the theology later. Thus the Jesus March idea was based on subjective feelings – and now the founders admit there is no New Testament precedent for what they are doing. BUT THAT DOESN'T MATTER, they say! What is important is unity and agreement amongst the participants about what they are trying to achieve.

Amongst other things, Roger Forster says the March is claiming territory for God in prayer by pulling down the strongholds of Satan. But in doing so, he admits THEY DON'T REALLY KNOW WHAT THEY'RE DOING!!

> *We don't know* how to engage totally the spiritual forces of darkness that are vested in the structures of society...

> *We don't know* what happens when we declare the victory of Jesus into the cosmos – what we do know is something happens. [emphasis added] ⁶

What does happen? We shall see.

Spiritual Warfare was the aim from the very beginning. Before the marches began, the founders were already inclined that way:

LYNN GREEN: (1985) – "By now we were beginning to think that the principalities, powers, and spiritual strongholds had historical roots, so we looked into different parts of London where we felt there was a stronghold of greed....."⁷

ROGER FORSTER: (1974) – "We began to notice that a change took place in the heavens – the awareness was subjective, but others also noticed it."⁸

GRAHAM KENDRICK: (1983) – "I became interested in the dynamics of praise and its relation to prayer and spiritual warfare – I became convinced that God releases his power as people praise."[9]

GERALD COATES: (1987) "The aim was to mobilize Christians to proclaim the name of Jesus and to pronounce the defeat of the spiritual forces entrenched in the capital"[10]

The focus of the Jesus March is not so much the salvation of individual people, but territorial, geographic salvation!

This is accomplished by pulling down the spiritual rulers that God in His wisdom permits to remain in place. Also, it is pertinent to ask WHAT will replace these spiritual rulers, supposing they can be pulled down? Roger Forster believes that an elite corps of Christians is being trained up for that role!

In order to challenge the spiritual forces effectively, the prayers of the participants of the March For Jesus were scripted. The script for the first March said this:

> We trust that today will be the beginning of a greater visibility to the principalities and powers of the manifold wisdom of God – we are not on a ramble, but tackling grave concerns, while *seeking to effect some serious changes in the heavenlies.*[11] [emphasis added]

Within six months that change took effect, they say. On Black Monday 19th October 1987 the Stock Market crashed in London and New York and billions were wiped off the value of shares. By the end of that week, share prices dropped 102 billion pounds. "We praised God that changes were taking place," their book proudly states. (**March For Jesus** page 40)

Bankrupcies, redundancies, financial ruin, suicides – was this the fruit of the Jesus March? Let's not forget that three days earlier, the infamous hurricane had hit the South-East, felling a million trees and wrecking thousands of homes. A few weeks later, London suffered the notorious fireball disaster at King's Cross Tube Station in November of that year – yes, it certainly was a year when something happened! Did London become a less immoral or greedy city as a result? Was there revival? Did people turn to God in repentance? NO.   Are we a more God-fearing nation after six years of marching? NO. Crime figures continue to rise; pornography, drugs, abortion – all are worse than ever. There has been no national repentance or profound social change, quite the reverse!

The Kingdom Factor

A terrible misunderstanding of the Kingdom and of biblical eschatology lies at the base of this kind of thinking. The Bible speaks, primarily, of a FUTURE literal Kingdom: the glorious kingly reign of the Messiah after His return to this earth. (Matt 25:31- 34) There can be no Kingdom rule on earth without the presence of the Lord Jesus Christ, for the Kingdom is in Him and with Him.

Although there is a spiritual sense in which born-again believers have a foretaste of the Kingdom, that is only because of their association and unity with Jesus Christ. (Col 1:13) There is still a future Kingdom reality to be experienced, even for Christians, who are waiting for their Day of Redemption. (Heb 4:1,9) The unsaved cannot enter the Kingdom of God, either through their own righteousness or by Church membership. The only entrance is by spiritual birth:

Except a man be born again, he cannot see the kingdom of God. ***(John 3:3)***

Flesh and blood cannot inherit the kingdom of God. ***(1 Cor 15:50)***

What folly, then, to encourage the unsaved to obey God on the understanding that they are participating in the establishment of the worldwide Kingdom of God!

Uniting For The Kingdom

Unity is being pushed as THE requirement for completing the Church's supposed task of discipling all nations before the return of Christ. An article by Glenn Myers, titled "The Network Revolution" appeared in the March 1994 issue of the UK Christian magazine "Renewal." It began by pointing out that "only the whole Church has enough resources to reach the whole world," and said that uncoordinated efforts by local churches were **fatally flawed** because of their lack of unity.

The Jesus March and spiritual warfare events are designed to bring all denominations together in unity – **unity is the key**. The organisers believe Christ cannot come until there is full visible unity in the Church. Anyone who stands in the way is accused of destroying this unity – and that's also why doctrine is thrown out. Doctrine divides, they say – so let's ignore the scriptures and concentrate on love and unity.

Those who dare to raise points of doctrine are called nit-picking fundamentalists. Gerald Coates says:

> **Doctrinal unity is important in terms of the foundations of our faith, but it seems everyone who comes together on doctrinal unity ends up splitting....Then there are those who strive for methodological unity –** *this nit-picking fundamentalist evangelical approach to scripture that asks questions like –* **"Where is marching in the Bible?" Methods are important, but we are not primarily looking for methodological unity. We are primarily looking for relational unity – a display of love, unity, and joy."**[12]

There is a ban on examining the scriptures – because it shows up the shaky foundation of the whole scheme. To cover up the poverty of their theology, such teachers hide behind one or two texts plucked out of the Bible, such as "judge not lest ye be judged" and "touch not the Lord's anointed." Employing personal criticism as their weapon, they accuse brothers and sisters of unloving attitudes while backing away from the real issue – the correct understanding and use of scripture.

Francis Frangipane devoted a whole chapter to people he calls "fault-finders," in his book on taking the cities by spiritual warfare. These are the spanners in Restoration's well-oiled machinery, because they are "hindering the next move of God," according to Frangipane. These people are planted by Satan, he says, and he accuses them of being possessed by a "faultfinder demon,"

> **To mask the diabolical nature of its activity, the faultfinder (demon) will often garb its criticisms in religious clothing. Under the pretence of protecting sheep from a gnat-sized error in doctrine, it forces them to swallow a camel-sized error of loveless correction.**[13]

I wonder if Paul was possessed by such a demon when he corrected Peter (Gal 2:11) or whether Timothy was a fault-finder for "**commanding some that they teach no other doctrine but the Word of God**" (1 Tim 1:3). The scriptures were given to us for "doctrine, **reproof**, correction and instruction in righteousness" (2 Tim 3:16). Are we now forbidden to use them for this?

In my experience, most correction has been delivered gently and lovingly, as the Bible commands, by those whom the Lord has commissioned as watchmen. It has kept to its remit of scriptural exegesis, and not wandered off into groundless personal attacks. But in calling these watchmen demonized accusers of the brethren, Frangipane deflects from himself and his militant teachings any proper discussion of their theology.

And if any DO dare to question – then what?

• They are excommunicated – made outcasts in their own fellowships, their own neighbourhoods and amongst their own former friends.

• They are cursed by the elders, who pronounce the judgment of God (as they see it) upon opponents. This can actually result in tragedies and torments for the people at the receiving end of such curses.

• They suffer the new charismatic inquisition – the visit of the elders.

• They are openly reviled from the pulpits, denounced as critical, judgmental, and unloving.

- They are called heresy-hunters.
- They are called jezebels, and antichrists, having the wrong spirit – because they oppose the bringing in of the global kingdom.
- They are marked for judgment, and told that they are damned to hell – because they are opposing the great new move of God.

Paul Crouch of TBN, possibly the most influential religious TV network in the world, headed his October 1993 newsletter – **Blessed With Cursings**.

In it, he labels those who hold up current teachings to the light of scripture (for example Hank Hanagraaff) as wolves amongst the flock, false prophets, and false teachers who bring in "damnable heresies." To Paul Crouch, the heretics are those who "attack" (as he calls it) the Word-of-Faith teachers. Not content with name-calling, he goes on to damn these biblical apologists to hell.

He quotes 2 Peter 2:3 which says "their damnation slumbers not", and says that for sinful America and "heretics" alike **there is coming a curse so final and irreversible** that God not only gives them up but sends upon them strong delusion that they might be damned. (2 Thess 2:11-12).

But the future for the kingdom-builders is very different, he claims. No plagues will touch THEM – the death angel will pass over THEM, and – when this **blood-washed throng** finally realizes who **we are**, and arises as that **mighty army** that **no man can number**, His kingdom will finally **come**.

Are you ready for our finest hour? Will you **move out** when our Commander calls? The call is ringing out even NOW across the land: **"Arise my people. The land is before you. Move forward in my name and possess the waste places for my kingdom and glory...GO forth and Conquer in My strength and Name, saith the Lord of Hosts!"** [Emphasis in original].

Dear saints, the situation is now very serious. The hour is late, and the net is closing. We have reached the moment when the scriptures are being fulfilled, and "Woe to those who call evil good, and good evil" (Is 5:20). Those who love the truth and feed on the Word are called heretics – ready for damnation – but the "mighty army" who are determined to fly in the face of prophecy and establish the earthly kingdom before the coming of Christ are called the beloved of God.

Following in the footsteps of Rome, they denounce their critics as hell-bound heretics. They are the new Crusaders who show no mercy, for their goal is world dominion. Will they then, as Rome did, mount an INQUISITION to search out, test, and eliminate the so-called "antichrists", these trouble-makers who destroy unity and dare to challenge their plan?

THEY WILL! This is their belief and aim. Ulf Ekman, a Word-of-Faith teacher has said,

> The church of the nineties will not be a weak church, it will be a strong church, so strong that some people will say there is no love in it..but there will be love in it – a love of purity and right order in the *church that will eliminate rebellion—it will be a forceful church, a kingly church, an influential and an attacking church – even a military church* single-minded in purpose, zealous, and absolutely fanatical.[14] [emphasis added]

Some far-out Christians have even proposed capital punishment as God's judgment for rebellion, once they have installed the kingdom of God on earth. One such reconstructionalist, R.J. Rushdoony, says:

> If men will not obey God, then they will not obey men; they will then require the gallows and the gun as the necessary instruments of order..[15]

The new breed believe they are the feet of Jesus, destined to crush God's enemies underfoot. Francis Frangipane quotes Psalm 110 – ("The Lord said to my Lord, sit at my right hand until I make thine enemies a footstool for thy feet") – and commented that **the CHURCH is the feet of Jesus** – God is supposed to have promised Jesus that: "I will train your feet, and use them to tread upon and crush your enemies."[16]

Judging from the preceding quotes, it's not hard to guess just WHO are the enemies of this new super-Church.

Networking

Given the goal of reaching the whole world by the year 2000, Glenn Myers – a writer for WEC International – offered networking as the answer. He explains in his article [in the March 1994 issue **Renewal**] that the knots in the net are local churches, linked together by shared information and events.

Roger Forster goes much further. He sees a supernatural dimension to the net; it has energy lines forged between local churches that pulsate with "Holy Spirit Kingdom power", and draw all around into its web.

"Our task is to network the world", he says, "Each local church is like a knot in the net from which it emits, extends, and exerts Holy Spirit Kingdom power over the immediate territory."[17] In the book, **March For Jesus** the power-lines that are to link the network together were seen in vision. During the YWAM Torch Run in 1988, committee member John Pressdee saw a picture of spiritual power-lines:

> He saw two heavy-duty power-cables that were to be joined on 16th September when the two groups of walkers converged on London to light one giant flame. He said, "there would be a prophetic coming together of these two prayer cables and *the power would begin to flow. I saw it as the powering up of a great network, not just on a temporary basis, but a whole network coming alive with current flowing throughout the country* – a network of churches to create a permanent spiritual national grid."[18] [emphasis added]

On the first International March for Jesus, May 1992, one of the March's four founders Gerald Coates said:

> The electricity grid throughout Britain is a symbol of the prayer walk team's prayers for networks and relationships to grow among Christians. These would become a *spiritual grid system* through which the Holy Spirit might flow to flood the nation with the light of the gospel. Churches uniting in prayer would spread this revival power, like the pylons and high-tension wires, *carrying power throughout the land. And now, together with other nations of Europe and beyond, we are plugging into a much greater gospel power-grid.* This one could

stretch across the globe with the pylons and power cables of united prayer, praise, and proclamations.[19]

One of the most disturbing features of this vision of the Global network is that, according to Forster, it "enmeshes everything, good AND evil", but the evil is brought into the Kingdom net for the purposes of **judgment**. Quoting the dragnet parable of Matt 13:47-50, Forster says that, "Jesus will pull in the net of his kingdom when it covers the world, enmeshing everything, good and evil."[20]

This enmeshing of all things and all peoples in the church network seems to be describing recruitment and church membership rather than spiritual rebirth. Are the new movements for evangelism more concerned about numerical superiority than true converts? Are they aiming at faithful disciples for their creed, rather than faithful followers of Jesus Christ?

The last time that a Church had so much world dominion was when Rome ruled the world. Then, it was often fatal not to be a faithful member of that system and the only "salvation" possible was through that Church. At that time, there was indeed a network around the world that enmeshed all things, good and evil.

Rome's net was plucked from her hands by the Protestant Reformation – but are we now witnessing the resurrection of that beast, energetically aided and abetted by Charismatic Protestants?

2. Does the Bible indicate a global revival before the return of Christ?

Obviously, our answer to this question will affect our response to national evangelism, since no one will embark on an intensive campaign to achieve the impossible. I have found, though, that the answer people give is more likely to be based on personal hopes and ambitions and on wishful thinking than on strict attention to Bible prophecy.

The Way to Calvary

With God all things are possible, and I do not want to rule out the possibility of a harvest of souls before the End. Yet there are clear indications that the conditions prevailing just before the Return of Christ are anything but conducive to global revival. They even militate against moderate success for the gospel.

This is something we all find hard to accept. At the prospect of the Church of the endtimes following Jesus to Gethsemane and Calvary, we tend to speak with the voice of Peter:

Be it far from thee, Lord: this shall not be unto thee. But [Jesus] turned, and said unto Peter, Get thee behind me, Satan: thou art an offence unto me: for thou savourest not the things that be of God, but those that be of men.

Then said Jesus unto his disciples,

If any [man] will come after me, let him deny himself, and take up his cross, and follow me. For whosoever will save his life shall lose it: and whosoever will lose his life for my sake shall find it. For what is a man profited, if he shall gain the whole world, and lose his own soul? Or what shall a man give in exchange for his soul? **(Matthew 16:22-26)**

Peter was motivated by the same sort of human thinking that besets us all – it was focused on his own life and his own world. Faced with oppression, violence, injustice, paganism, and every kind of evil, Peter longed to see God do something "positive"; he wanted to see his enemies routed and all peoples brought into submission to God. He wanted Jesus immediately to overthrow Satan and all his forces, and he couldn't see how God would have it otherwise – yet, bafflingly, Jesus walked on towards torture and death, disappointing even his closest followers.

While Peter insisted on man's answer to evil, speaking with the voice of Satan, Jesus spoke with the voice of the Holy Spirit:

"Nevertheless not my will, but thine, be done." (Lu 22:42) In choosing to obey God the Father, rather than the rational desires of man, Jesus brought about the greatest victory every known. The same reasoning goes for His Body on earth. Once having accepted that God's plan really is better than ours, we can begin to see the prophecies of the End in a different light.

Endtimes Prophecy

Every indication is that the endtimes will be characterized by increasing lawlessness. All restraint to evil behaviour will be overthrown. (2 Tim 3) Eventually, all who are not found in the Book of Life will worship the Antichrist, and refuse to repent. (Rev 13:8) The Bible does not prophesy any interruption in this process to allow for national or global revival.

When asked to describe the signs of the End and of His return, rather than offer the hope of a glorious harvest of souls, Jesus spoke of deception, persecution, wars, violence, and catastrophes. (Matt 24:4-13) His focus was on the endurance needed by believers to withstand the pressures of those days, not on their victorious achievements.

It is often argued that Jesus also mentioned global evangelism as a sign of the endtimes. He said, "And this gospel of the kingdom shall be preached in all the world for a witness unto all nations; and then shall the end come." (Mt 24:14)

But several things could be said about that verse. Firstly, since Jesus' day, the gospel HAS been preached in all the world; secondly, the gospel mentioned here could be a specific one – "THIS gospel of the KINGDOM" – that is, the specific news of the coming Messiah and the events surrounding his return.

Thirdly, worldwide gospel preaching – even if it is prophesied – will not necessarily result in a harvest of millions (as promised by some). Though the Lord, in his mercy, may allow mankind one last warning, it seems from scripture that most people ignore it.

Scripture says that Jesus will not discover a thriving worldwide Christian kingdom on earth when He returns. (Luke 18:8) It tells us that "few" find the narrow path that leads to life. (Matt 7:14) All of this highlights the dangers of promising fantastic results from global or national evangelism.

3. What is the "gospel" preached at modern-day evangelistic events?

It is sad to have to ask this question. We ought to be able to trust Christian preachers to present the truth according to scripture. Seemingly, we cannot.

Since the Kingdom message is about transforming this earth and setting up the universal reign of Christ through his Church, the focus of the Restoration gospel reflects those aims.

The goal is to present Christianity as an answer to the world's problems – hence it dwells on **earthly desires** more than spiritual requirements. Gerald Coates sees it this way:

> **Our task is to make Jesus attractive and intelligible. Through words and deeds [social work] to build bridges of love because human beings are worth it, and in the hope that we might have the rich privilege of sharing our faith with them. In so doing, as people respond, the earth will fill up with reasonable people who have been given the ability to make peace rather than war, to be faithful rather than promiscuous, to bring heaven rather than hell into the world.**[21]

Clearly, flesh-debasing messages about sin, hell, and separation from the world are not going to do the job!

Rather than bring men and women under conviction for their sin and call them to repentance, today's preaching simply concentrates on all the advantages of belonging to Jesus. This results in what used to be called "rice-christians" who join the churches for what they can get – such as rice handouts in India.

Here is an illustration, borrowed from a recent newsletter:[22] A man travelling in an aircraft is offered a parachute by the stewardess and told it will give him a better flight. He is encouraged to put it on, but after a while notices not only that the other passengers are laughing at him, but also that the parachute has done nothing to improve his journey. It is cumbersome and heavy. So eventually he takes it off again.

A second man is told that the plane he is travelling on is certain to crash shortly. He will have to jump out at 25,000 feet. He is then offered the parachute and told it will save his life. He puts it on, and endures its heaviness and discomfort. He also ignores the whispering and pointing fingers of the others, because he is anticipating the crash and knows that he, at least, will be saved.

No illustration is perfect, and this has many flaws. But it says this: if we give people the impression that "putting on Christ" will improve their lives, then after a time, when the shine wears off, they will backslide and even accuse us of deceiving them. However, if we explain the penalty for sin, the fate of unbelievers, the coming judgment, and the crash shortly coming to this world, they will have all the more reason to take Christ for salvation, and rejoice in Him despite any hardship, persecution, or self-sacrifice entailed.

A self-centered gospel message is not only unbiblical, but it is dishonest. It leads people into false expectations for their future, and fails to point out the level of commitment involved. It also reduces Jesus Christ to a sort of coin-in-the-slot chocolate machine, standing ready to dispense goodies to all and sundry.

The effect of a self-oriented gospel is to produce selfish disciples of that creed, ever searching for more good things to enhance their lives. How many of the supposed "decisions" at large evangelistic meetings are of that kind? How many of these "converts" return to their old lives when the razzmatazz and excitement of the meeting is over? We are told only the number of inquirers at a meeting, not the fall-out rate, so we'll never know.

It can hardly be better expressed than in this extract:

> **A man may make a profession without every having his confidence in his own ability shattered; he has been told absolutely nothing of his need for a change of nature which is not within his own power, and consequently, if he does NOT experience such a radical change, he is not dismayed. He was never told it was essential, so he sees no reason to doubt whether he is a Christian. Indeed, the teaching he has come under consistently militates against such doubts arising. It is frequently said that a man who has made a decision with little**

evidence of a change of life may be a "carnal" Christian who needs instruction in holiness, or if the same individual should gradually lose his new-found interests, the fault is frequently attributed to lack of "follow-up", or prayer, or some other deficiency on the part of the Church. The possibility that these marks of worldliness and falling away are due to the absence of a saving experience at the outset is rarely considered.[23]

Before the end of these things, before Jesus comes to gather us, there will be so many subtle, devious and counterfeit events that our souls will cry "**Mercy!**" The deception is drawing nearer and nearer to the truth, until hardly any distinction can be drawn – yet there IS a difference.

This difference can always be found in the Word of God, our only foundation and plumb line.

False gospels look for a **solution** to this world's crisis situation, not an **escalation** into inevitable judgment. They preach the restoration of all things, not the **redemption** of individual souls. They seek a **new age** that involves converting most of the world's population, whereas the Bible prophesies **the kingdom reign of antichrist**, followed by dreadful judgments.

The true gospel says the problem is fallen man who needs a Saviour. The answer is to be born again of the Spirit and restored to God. Simple as that. Throughout all ages, in every nation at every time, this has been the gospel of God – calling men and women to repent, and to be reconciled to God the Father through Jesus Christ. This gospel does not need to be made more relevant, updated, modernized, or changed to suit present-day circumstances. Let's see what the Bible has to say about this.

Our Lord Jesus Christ gave himself for our sins, that he might ***deliver us from this present evil world****, according to the will of God and our Father: To whom [be] glory for ever and ever. Amen. I marvel that ye are so soon removed from him that called you into the grace of Christ unto another gospel: Which is not another; but there be some that trouble you, and would pervert the gospel of Christ. But though we, or an angel from heaven, preach any other* *gospel unto you than that which we have preached unto you,* **let him be accursed.** *(Gal 1:3b-8)*

Notice that Jesus died to DELIVER US from this present evil world – the Greek word used is ἐξαιρειν (EX-AIREIN), which means **to take away out of** (like Acts 7:34). God is going to take us out of here! It is not His intention to use the Church to solve this world's problems and to restore all things, as some now preach. Paul called that sort of distortion "another gospel" which is ACCURSED!

If the Apostle Paul saw fit to question a pseudo-gospel message that was leading believers astray, then surely we must do the same.

4. What is biblical evangelism?

We seem to think that what passes for "evangelism" today is the only possible expression of biblical gospel preaching. Are we forgetting that the salvation message has been preached for nearly two thousand years, more or less effectively? We should base our evangelism on the Bible accounts of preaching, and note how preaching has been conducted throughout the years of the Church age.

Since all gospel preaching must be directed and empowered by the Holy Spirit, let's look at His ministry.

John 16:8-11 *And when he is come, he will reprove the world of sin, and of righteousness, and of judgment: Of sin, because they believe not on me; Of righteousness, because I go to my Father, and ye see me no more; Of judgment, because the prince of this world is judged.*

Classic biblical preaching is that men and women are, firstly, convicted of their sin and rebellion against God, secondly, made to know their helplessness in the face of God's righteous judgment, and thirdly, urged to obtain the righteousness that is only found in Christ by repenting of their sin and believing on Him as their means of escape. (Acts 2:36-37)

None of this entails promises to improve their worldly lot. In fact, the early Christians would have been surprised if it did so – and even today in much of the world, becoming a Christian is tantamount to a death sentence! Yet, the conviction of sin and judgment can be so strong that it impels people to run to Jesus for salvation, even so.

Furthermore, without the activity of the Holy Spirit, without the drawing of God, no man or woman can come to the Lord. (John 6:44) Preaching is therefore not a matter of rhetoric, showmanship, persuasive words, or personal charm. (1 Cor 2:4) No amount of rousing music, stirring testimonies, or appeals to the emotions can create a convert in truth. That sort of worldly wisdom only leads to shallow conversions of the mind, not the heart.

Today's evangelism, too, vies with the world for entertainment value and excitement. Each meeting is carefully crafted to be as attractive as possible to the soul of man. So, when people are invited to commit themselves, they naturally associate this thrilling activity with Christianity, and their commitment is as much to the groups who organize the events as to their Lord. Needy people without much joy in their lives rarely shrink from joining up with an organization so powerful, so wealthy, so influential, and so entertaining. But would they think twice if they were told the truth?

The call of the gospel is to examine ourselves in the light of scripture and repent of our shortcomings; then to go to God for forgiveness and reconciliation. It is to "come to Christ", not to join the Church, or seek advice, blessing, provision, help or whatever we most need. In contrast to the shallow appeals of today, look at the invitation used by Spurgeon:

> Before you leave this place, breathe an earnest prayer to God, saying, 'God be merciful to me a sinner. Lord, I need to be saved. Save me! I call upon Thy name. Lord, I am guilty, I deserve Thy wrath. Lord, I cannot save myself. Lord, I would have a new heart and a right spirit, but what can I do? Lord, I can do nothing – come and work in me to do of Thy good pleasure. But I now do from my very soul call upon Thy name. Trembling, yet believing, I cast myself wholly upon Thee, O Lord. I trust the blood and righteousness of Thy dear Son. Lord, save me tonight, for Jesus' sake.'[24]

Conversion is more than a passing regret – it is an utter conviction of our helpless, lost and desperate condition before a righteous God. And salvation is more than a good feeling that comes from adopting a better way of life. It is receiving a new life altogether! The "old man" of the human nature MUST be put to death in Jesus before His eternal, victorious life can flood our spirits. Christianity is not an optional extra to be tacked onto our old way of life. Anyone who misses this point is unlikely to experience a true conversion.

Yet how many people will get the chance to hear these truths in the evangelistic meetings of today?

What then shall we do?

I have been saying for many months that the greatest danger will come when the prophecies of global revival **will seem to be fulfilled!** The danger is not at a time when the "restoration of all things" looks impossible – but when some sort of "revival" actually happens; when signs and wonders DO begin to break out, when thousands ARE flocking to join this "great move of God", and when it looks like the Kingdom of God really IS coming to pass upon the earth.

When that happens, we will all have a vital choice to make. Will we continue to believe in the endtime scenario as laid out in scripture – the antichrist, the tribulation, the rapture, the millennium, and so forth – or will we conclude that we must have been mistaken? Will we be persuaded to jump on the revival bandwagon, afraid to "miss out" – or will we stand firm on the Word of God, despite all temptation? These questions may decide our own personal walk, and the course of the Church as a whole.

Is there anything we can do to prepare ourselves for that crucial choice? Certainly. We must take a stand NOW on the Rock of our Salvation – the Lord Jesus – and on His Word. We must lay aside human concerns, human emotions, and human desires, and obey God alone. We must do as he says: – **"Take heed that no man deceive you"**, (Matt 24:4) and **"Watch ye therefore, and pray** always, that ye may be accounted worthy to escape all these things that shall come to pass." (Luke 21:36)

We can also be discerning about the teachings we hear and the company we keep. Spiritual Warfare, Global Evangelism, Restoration, Ecumenism – all these are challenged and exposed by the Word of God, so take everything to the Bible and CHECK IT OUT. Then obey the Lord's command with regard to false teachers. The Bible is clear. It says we are to REPROVE such people, (2 Tim 4:1-5) and if they refuse to be corrected then to WITHDRAW from them. (Eph 5:3-11) And in the meantime,

- Continue to work for God to the best of your ability, especially in leading others to know Him.
- Fellowship as often as you are able with those who truly love the Word and whose focus is the will of God. Beware exciting man-led ministries.
- Seriously check out your own spiritual condition, and identify error in your own life by asking the Lord for correction and guidance. Keep humble.
- Don't allow sin to ruin your walk with the Lord.
- Think seriously about the ways in which you thwart God's move in your life by pride, self-will, human desires, and emotional attachments – then work on eliminating these, and allowing God to be your Lord in all areas. Never be led by the flesh.
- Avoid all techniques to "hear the voice of God/sense God" and so on, that involve mental and spiritual passivity, (switching off). At all times be in control of your mind and body.
- Intensify your private prayer and Bible-study times, asking God to shed light on His Word.
- Commit yourself to know and obey the will of God at all times. This, above all, is vital.

1 Thes 5:23-24 And the very God of peace sanctify you wholly; and I pray God your whole spirit and soul and body be preserved blameless unto the coming of our Lord Jesus Christ. Faithful is he that calleth you, who also will do it.

Appendix Three References

1. Boyer, Paul, **When Time Shall Be No More.** Harvard University Press 1992. Page 303. Quoting David Chilton.
2. Mansell, David. "Changing The World God's Way." **Restoration Magazine.** Sept/Oct 1990.
3. Hosier, John. **Seeking The Kingdom.** Booklet. Word. 1990.
4. Kendrick, Forster, Coates, and Green. **March For Jesus.** Kingsway Publications UK 1992. Page 131.
5. Ibid. Page 135.
6. Ibid. Page 140.
7. Ibid. Page 17.
8. Ibid. Page 19.
9. Ibid. Page 24.
10. Ibid. Page 28.
11. Ibid. Page 37.
12. Ibid. Page 13.
13. Frangipane, Francis. **House of The Lord – God's Plan To Liberate Your City From Darkness.** Creation House USA 1991/Word UK 1992. Page 134.
14. "Faith That Takes A Nation." Address at Faith '90.
15. Eye, Mae, **A Call To Christian Jihad.** PO Box 19468, Sacramento. Page 103. Quoting Rushdoony. The Institutes Of Biblical Law. Vol 1. 1973.
16. Frangipane, Francis. **Charisma Magazine.** July, 1993.
17. Forster, Roger. Foreword to **Territorial Spirits.** C. Peter Wagner. Sovereign World 1991.
18. **March for Jesus.** Page 66.
19. Ibid. Page 115.
20. Roger Forster. Ibid.
21. Coates, Gerald. "Back To Basics" article. **Christian Herald** newspaper. May, 1993.
22. Comfort, Ray. Excerpt from "Hell's Best Kept Secret" in **Sword & Trumpet** newsletter, (Nov/Dec 93) PO Box 870, Chandler, Texas 75758, USA.
23. Murray, Iain. **The Forgotten Spurgeon.** (London 1966).

24. Murray. Ibid.

Appendix Four

Gnosticism: What is it?

I Timothy 6:20-21 O Timothy, keep that which is committed to thy trust, avoiding profane and vain babblings, and oppositions of science falsely so called; which some professing have erred concerning the faith. Grace be with thee. Amen.

Lord God of Abraham, God of Isaac, and God of Jacob and Israel, who are the Father of our Lord Jesus Christ, the God who through the abundance of thy mercy, hast a favour toward us, that we should know thee...give to every reader of this book to know thee, that thou art God alone, to be strengthened in thee, and to avoid every heretical and impious doctrine... Irenaeus, *Against Heresies 111:6:4*

There has been a persistent challenge to the true faith of the Apostles, down through history, that has often recurred, by the name of Gnosticism. Like Paul's thorn, Gnosticism has oft troubled the church, periodically being prevailed over, but never fully removed. It resurfaces from generation to generation, swaying from fringe to forefront, in different packages, but espousing basically the same lies. To this day, Gnosticism is a valid challenge to the church, and seems to be enjoying a revival.

History and Definition

If you had visited a first, second, or third century city, say Ephesus, and asked for directions to the Gnostic church, you would have been met with a blank stare. Gnosticism was never an organized movement, rather, it's always been a loosely knit system of thought, a philosophy. At some points in church history, there were probably Gnosticly influenced people in every church. Gnosticism was already in existence when the church was founded, having sprung from Greek philosophy. It was a syncretistic religion, influencing paganism and even Judaism. By the time the epistles were written, the Gnostic leaven was already corrupting parts of the church. Many of the writings of the apostles were given to combat Gnosticism, notably; I John, Colossians, and I Corinthians. The apostles and early fathers recognized it as a serious threat to the true faith (orthodoxy), and withstood it vigorously. May we also be given grace to discern and withstand the renewed strains of Gnosticism and defend the faith which was once and for all given to the saints.

The name, Gnosticism (pronounced *nos-tis-ism*), comes from the Greek word Gnosis, meaning knowledge. An A̲gnostic is one who claims he doesn't know, the prefix A̲ meaning non. But a Gnostic is a "knowing one!" The idea is that there is a gnosis, knowledge, that one must possess, that either saves you, or brings you into spiritual realization and fulfilment. The Gnostic believed that he had received an esoteric (hidden) knowledge, that most of the "run of the mill Christians" had not received. Gnosticism in a nutshell, is salvation by knowledge, or spiritual experience, (oneness with God) by knowledge. The emphasis though is that it is esoteric knowledge, only revealed to those "special people" that God chooses. This may explain Gnosticism's recurring appeal, everybody wants to be "in the know." It goes back to the Garden. The first couple were offered enlightenment and equality with God, through the "forbidden" knowledge. Could there be anything wrong with such "self improvement?" There has to be some "secret" to intimacy and oneness with God, simple faith in the Gospel and repentance, are too simplistic for some intellectuals.

What is This Gnosis?

The ultimate Gnostic revelation is this, God can be found within you. One way or another it always comes back to this. Through the Gnosis, you can discover God within, or Christ in you (individually), or the Divine Spark that is in each one of us. All of this, in whatever form, is a rehash of Satan's Lie to Adam and Eve in the Garden. For example, here's a portion of a Kenneth Copeland tape which brings this Gnosis out so clearly.

When you were born again, Peter said it just as plain, he said, "We are partakers of the divine nature." That nature is life eternal in absolute perfection. And that was imparted, injected into your spirit man, and you have that imparted into you by God, just the same as you imparted into your child the nature of humanity. That child wasn't born a whale! It was born a human. Isn't that true? Well, now, you don't have a human, do you? You are one. You don't have a god in you. You are one.[1]

The idea that man is a little "g" god, or created in God's class of being is Gnosticism, rehashed and revived. The present gospel of Gnosticism is that, though Adam and Eve and all of us, were created in "God's class" of being, when man sinned, he fell "below the God class."[2] Jesus came to redeem us and restore us back to our rightful dominion, as little gods. As Copeland says, "And I say this with all respect, so that I don't upset you too bad. But, I say it anyway: When I read the Bible where He says "I AM," I just smile and say, "Yes, I AM too."[3] On a recent nationwide television show, Paul Crouch and Ken Copeland had this exchange of doctrinal discussion:

P.C.: [God] doesn't even draw a distinction between himself and us.
K.C.: Never, Never! You never can do that in a covenant relationship.
P.C.: Do you know what else that has settled, then tonight? This hue and cry and controversy that has been spawned by the devil to try and bring dissension within the body of Christ, that we are gods. I am a little god!
K.C.: Yes! Yes!
Jan Crouch: Absolutely! He gave us His name!
P.C.: I have His name. I'm one with Him. I'm in covenant relations – I am a little god! Critics, be gone!
K.C.: You are anything that He is.
P.C.: Yes.

This was the essence of Gnostical teaching that alarmed the early church, it should alarm us today. Unfortunately, we are living in a spiritual climate that is more concerned about disunity or lack of love than heresy and doctrines of demons. The Charismatic/Pentecostal church is especially endangered by this unfortunate position. May God help us by raising fearless leadership who will instill in us a love for the truth!

155

The Gnostic Obsession with Self

A favourite Gnostic proof text is "the Kingdom of God is within you." The correct view of this verse is, in your midst, I (Jesus) am the very embodiment of the Kingdom, here standing among you! But, for example, in the ancient, Gnostic gospel of Thomas, Jesus is quoted as saying, "When you come to know yourself, then you will be known." In his excellent book, **Against the Protestant Gnostics**, Phillip Lee stated the Gnostic philosophy quite succinctly when he said, "The Gnostic illumination, enables persons not so much to see their own reflection in the being of God, as to see the being of God in their own reflection."[5] In another ancient Gnostic writing, Jesus supposedly says, "As you see yourselves in water or mirror, so see you me in yourselves." The Gnostics have everything reversed! We were made to reflect God's attributes and glory! God isn't there, within us, to reflect us back to self!

There are many religious personalities who held to this kind of philosophy. M. Scott Peck, a popular psychologist, whose best selling books can be found in many Christian bookstores, said in one of his books,

> **God wants us to become Himself...We are growing toward godhood, God is the goal of Evolution.**[6]

Fred Price, a pastor in California and an internationally known author and conference speaker, has been quoted as saying,

> **Man is the only creation of God that is in God's class...I believe that through these scriptures we can very clearly see that God made man a god.**[7]

As you can see, Gnosticism is driven by the desire to elevate man to God's class, and the idea that through this "hidden knowledge" rediscovered, we can find God within us. Thus, Gnosticism is very self-centered. The pursuit for God is turned inward. The idea is to find out "who you are in Christ", and "what you have in Him". To a Gnostic, discovering God is discovering self.

The Gnostic gospel of Thomas, has Jesus saying, "Whoever finds himself is superior to the world." Another Gnostic document says, "The kingdom of heaven is within you and whosoever shall know himself shall find it." Contrast this with Matthew 16:24-25.

***Matthew 16:24-25** Then said Jesus unto his disciples, If any man will come after me, let him deny himself, and take up his cross, and follow me. For whosoever will save his life shall lose it: and whosoever will lose his life for my sake shall find it.*

Even if it is concerned with spiritual well being, self preoccupation is counter to Christianity. Yet, go to any Christian bookstore and you'll find 75% of the books are concerned with the development, nurture, understanding, and healing of the self.

Gnosticism is Highly Individualized

If indeed God dwells within you, or you are a little god, then consequently you don't need anyone else. Thus Gnostic spirituality is highly individualistic. Union with God, within you, is the only worthy goal to a Gnostic. The church only has value to the extent that it transmits the Gnosis. Every Gnostic "outgrows" the church at some point in his personal relationship with Christ. The church gives you the milk, not the meat, the Gnostics say. Since God dwells within, the search for God ultimately becomes a search for self. Finding out who you are in Christ and what your rights and privileges and power is in Christ is a self-centered pursuit!

The present interpretation of much New Testament scripture has even taken a Gnostic twist at this very point. Ours is a highly individualized understanding of God's promises. We read I John 4:4, and conclude, He is in me, the Greater One is in me! Or we read II Corinthians 1:20 and say, Yes! All of the promises of God are mine! I have even been in worship services(?) where the scripture, "Know ye not ye are the temple of the Holy Ghost?" was individualized. The people actually sang, "Yes I know, yes I know, I am the temple, I am the temple of the Holy Ghost." The song went

157

on to proclaim, "I'm filled with power, filled with praise, filled with glory."!!?! Our use of scripture in song tells us volumes about ourselves and what we believe. The antidote would be a return to the idea that the promises are realized in a corporate sense. Christ is the greater one in the midst of us! The promises have been given to the body of Christ, which is the temple of the Holy Ghost, the dwelling place of God by the Spirit!

A beaming Christian convert, affected by the "Faith Movement," gave me a testimony. "Pastor, I woke up this morning feeling sick, but I laid my hands on myself and was healed!" Now that's modern Gnosticism, "I have all the power within, God lives in me," or as one faith man said, "The fullness of the Godhead dwells in me, because Christ is in me." The fullness of the Godhead dwelt in Christ and Christ alone. You aren't Christ. The New Testament teaching is that each of us have been given a measure. The individualized mindset is not the mindset that the apostles wrote the New Testament in! We need a renewed emphasis on the corporate nature of Christian faith. The Gnostic tends to become self sufficient.

Nowhere in the Bible is Jesus referred to as anyone's "personal Lord and Saviour". It is understood that upon salvation, you enter into the covenant community of God. Your inheritance is "in the saints". As Calvin said in his commentary on Ephesians, "He errs who desires to grow by himself...just so, if we wish to belong to Christ, let no man be anything for himself: but let us all be whatever we are for each other."

I Peter 2:9 But ye are a chosen generation, a royal priesthood, a holy nation, a peculiar people; that ye should show forth the praises of him who hath called you out of darkness into his marvellous light.

Elitism

Jude warned of those who would separate themselves above all the rest of the Christians, who are sensual and have not the Spirit. The Gnostics were very elitist, having divided the human race into three categories or levels.

At the very lowest level of human existence were the Somatics, from the Greek word for body – Soma. The Somatics lived their whole lives at the bodily level, eating, sleeping, making love, feeling sick and dying. The Gnostics despised these, for they felt they were above all of that. In Gnostic thought, the material world and the human body are evil, only spirit is good. A Gnostic, unlike an orthodox Christian, was not on a pilgrimage through the physical world, en route to heaven, rather he was attempting to escape this world, by turning within to the Spirit. I will develop this idea further on in the book.

On a slightly higher place were the Psychics. Now this word had nothing to with ESP. The Greek word ψυχη (Psuche) means, the soul. Psychics were those content to live life on the level of the mind, intellect, emotion or idea. Living in "head knowledge." To the Gnostic, the vast majority of the professing church lived at this low level. The Gnostics looked down on the Psychics, but believed that some of them could receive the Gnosis. Ironically, the Gnostics, who glorify a kind of salvation by knowledge, don't really value objective, doctrinal knowledge. Their knowledge is subjective, "revelation knowledge," as it is currently called. One modern Gnostic has said, "God isn't looking for people to understand the Bible, he just wants to find people who will believe it." How do you pit understanding against believing? And yet Gnostics do this often.

I Corinthians 8:1-3 Now as touching things offered to idols, we know that we all have knowledge. Knowledge puffeth up, but charity edifieth. And if any man think that he knoweth any thing, he knoweth nothing yet as he ought to know. But if any man love God, the same is known of him.

I John 5:20 And we know that the Son of God is come, and hath given us an understanding, that we may know him that is true, and we are in him that is true, even in his Son Jesus Christ. This is the true God, and eternal life.

At the highest level, are the Gnostikoi or Pneumatics, (from pneuma, spirit). These are the spiritual ones, who possess the revelation knowledge that lifts them above the rest of Christendom. As it was in the first, second and third centuries, so it is now. The plain meaning of scripture is too shallow for some, who always want to go deeper, read between the lines, or allegorically interpret everything in the Bible. Gnostics love to find totally unique interpretations of commonly understood scriptures. The Gnostic teacher wants to be able to say, like Jesus, "You have heard that it has been said by them of old time...but I say to you..." or in other words, "The church traditionally has taught it this way, but in the actual Greek, it says..." Charismatic preachers are all too often succumbing to this "Gnostic climate," where people are so eager to hear a new thing. Visions, dreams, revelations, supposed Greek and Hebrew words, prophecies, are all being used to foist on people deviant and errant interpretations of scripture. "The time has come when they will not endure sound doctrine, but are heaping to themselves teachers..." Beware when the basic tenants of the Apostles Creed, the Gospels, Epistles or Revelation no longer satisfy you. Isn't Christ sufficient?

The Gnostic is never content to be a mere human being, nor even just a Christian disciple. The ordinary "run of the mill" Christian has their faith in the plain meaning of scripture, but that's not enough for the Gnostic. Since salvation and spiritual development come by receiving the esoteric knowledge, than those who have this knowledge are exalted above the "average" Christian. How many times have I heard in faith churches, the condescending, "You have to understand, the average Christian hasn't had the revelation that we've been given." What is the matter with worshipping God as a creation, a man, redeemed, certainly, but still a man within limitations, a beginning and an end? The new

Gnostics wouldn't want that, they have to be "cutting edge," God's end time warriors, even the "Manchild Company!"

Dualism

Gnostic thought is highly dualistic, which means that in their world view, they see a sharp contrast between two mutually exclusive spheres of existence. On the one hand, there is light (spirit), the unseen realm, which is pure good. Opposed to this is the darkness, (flesh, matter), which is the seen realm, pure evil. In fact, some Gnostics went so far as to teach that it was an evil God who created the physical world! To a Gnostic, salvation means release from the physical world, including the body, through Gnosis of the divinity within you. This is essentially a religion of escape, but also of human exaltation.

The Gnostic view of the human body gives a prime example. Sine the body is physical, it must be evil. It is either evil or irrelevant. If it is evil, than it's functions are necessary evils. Eating, drinking, defecation, sleep and especially sex, all are evil. To advance to oneness with God, you must abstain from these activities as much as possible. This practice is called Asceticism, the harsh use of the body with the intent to develop the spirit. Many Gnostics were attempting to escape their body. The celibacy of priests is not a Christian concept, it is Gnostic. So is Monasticism. The religious hang ups about sex and eating are Gnostic influences. Remember Jesus' description of himself, "The Son of Man came eating and drinking." Gnostics are actually offended at the incarnation.

Orthodoxy gives us a healthier perspective. The God who created the material world and called it good is the God who actually came to us in the flesh, fully experienced humanity, and died on a real, wooden, cross. If you had run your hand up that cross on that day, you would have a hand full of splinters.

Ephesians 5:29 For no man ever yet hated his own flesh; but nourisheth and cherisheth it, even as the Lord the church.

No one can hate his flesh and remain psychologically healthy. Sin isn't located in the flesh anyway. It is our stubborn will that rebels against God. God will resurrect our body one day, because a full human experience is both spiritual and physical. "The Son of Man came both eating and drinking!" As a human being, I am a unity, I have a finite, created spirit, soul, and body. How could my spirituality not affect my body? Isn't what I do with by body a reflection of the way that I think? To be fully human is as much to laugh at a joke as to worship, as much to play with your children as to feel guilty, get angry, be vindicated, forgiven, eat food, make love, pray in tongues, and speak the word. It is folly to categorize human experience into spirit/material.

Colossians 2:20-23 *Wherefore if ye be dead with Christ from the rudiments of the world, why, as though living in the world, are ye subject to ordinances, (touch not; taste not; handle not; which all are to perish with the using;) after the commandments and doctrines of men? Which things have indeed a shew of wisdom in will worship, and humility, and neglecting of the body; not in any donor to the satisfying of the flesh.*

One ridiculous example was a man called Simon Styletes. A Stylite is a pillar, from whence Simon got his name. This 4th century Gnostic, gained renown after climbing a pillar and staying on top of it for 37 years, through rain, snow, night, and day! A ladder was set up for visitors and his disciples delivered food to him in a basket. And people thought he was spiritual! This is certainly not Christianity! True Christianity has never been about escaping the human body. Such a so-called "holy life" is nothing more than a harsher form of self-absorption!

But this dualism is a pendulum that swings both ways, from Asceticism to lasciviousness. The error that spirit is good and flesh is evil also resulted in the idea that what the body did was irrelevant, all that mattered was "Who are you in the Spirit Man." What does it matter that you are a fornicator, the physical part of you isn't the real you anyway! You are the righteousness of God in

Christ, remember? Supposedly, in the real you, the Spiritman, you are absolutely sinless.

Sharply dividing human identity is an error with huge consequences. I realize that I Thess 5:23 categorizes the spirit, soul and body, but that idea is distorted when it results in a compartmentalizing of your life. It is not true that the body is not you, the spirit is. To be a complete human being in the truest sense of the word is to be spirit, soul, and body. What a person does with his body is just as much a reflection of who they are, as how they think, and what their deepest motives are. In other words, you can't separate a person from what they do. Nor is it true that the reborn human spirit is perfect and in "God's class of being" as faith teachers spuriously hold forth.

John's Remedy for Gnosticism

First John chapter one touches on this by articulating three Gnostic statements and responding with orthodox doctrine.

I John 1:6 If we say that we have fellowship with Him and walk in darkness, we lie and do not the truth.

This counters the Gnostic spiritualization of actual righteousness, which would say, it doesn't matter what I do, just who I am in Christ. It does too matter.

I John 1:8 If we say we have no sin, we deceive ourselves and the truth is not in us.

The god-like perfection of the "spirit-man" is refuted in this verse. Every one has some element of sin to deal with.

I John 1:10 If we say that we have not sinned we make Him a liar and His word is not in us.

I have actually heard Word and Faith preachers say, "Drop that sinner label! You are a new creature, you are not a sinner saved by grace!" Oh yes I am.

I John 2:3-5 And hereby we do know that we know him, if we keep his commandments. He that saith, I know him, and keepeth not his commandments, is a liar, and the truth is not in him. But whoso keepeth his word, in him verily is the love of God perfected: hereby we know that we are in him.

Gnosticism is notoriously antinomian (anti-law). Gnostics believe that because of their mystical knowledge which has helped them escape the material world, they are not under any law at all. There are no moral obligations for them, they are 'free in Christ". John is telling us not to be confused, it's not that salvation is by the law, it isn't. But if you really have been saved, and love God, you'll be concerned about His commandments, but out of love, not duty! I don't care one lick about Jewish ceremonial law or food laws, but I am deeply concerned about the ten commandments which shall never pass away. Gnosticism has so affected modern Charismatics, that anytime any minister proclaims obedience to God, the cry rings out "legalism!". There is a new Exodus, to a "freer" church. When was the last time you heard a sermon expounding the ten commandments?

I John 2:12-14 I write unto you, little children, because your sins are forgiven you for his name's sake. I write unto you, fathers, because you have known him that is from the beginning. I write unto you, young men, because ye have overcome the wicked one. I write unto you, little children, because ye have known the Father. I have written unto you, fathers, because ye have known him that is from the beginning. I have written unto you, young men, because ye are strong, and the word of God abideth in you, and ye have overcome the wicked one.

To the Gnostic, Pistis, simple faith, is dull, humdrum, and insufficient. "Give me some meat." So you have preachers trying to be unique, to give some new twist to a commonly understood verse, trying to get "revelation". John is telling the church at every level of growth, children, young men, fathers, you know Him already, don't get conned into thinking that your simple faith in forgiveness, the scripture, the Gospel, and creation, is insufficient to know Him by. Gnostics with their dreams, visions, mystical experiences, are always conning the simple into exchanging what God gave them for something "deeper". They think they know something the rest of the Church hasn't come into yet. Are you a Gnostic? Have you been influenced by Gnostic thought?

I John 5:19-21 And we know that we are of God, and the whole world lieth in wickedness. And we know that the Son of God is come, and hath given us an understanding, that we may know him that is true, and we are in him that is true, even in his Son Jesus Christ. This is the true God, and eternal life. Little children, keep yourselves from idols. Amen.

The best way to sum up Gnostic error is by way of contrast with Orthodox Christianity. As First John sets forth, they claim to know something, but, we also claim to know. The difference is that Gnostics emphasize subjective knowledge, mystical experience, a knowledge pertaining to self. Orthodox Christianity is based on objective knowledge, outside of self, what God has done for us in Christ in history, and of course, how it applies to me, by faith. To an orthodox Christian, scripture in its plain meaning is essential, it is the self revelation of God. To a Gnostic, scripture is not necessarily essential, although it could apply to me in some sense, especially if spiritualized. A Gnostic would ask, what does the giant represent in David and Goliath? What does the flood really represent? To an Orthodox Christian, the meaning is plain, God has acted in human history, and He will act again in time, space, history – period!

A Return to True Humanity

What it boils down to is this, the Gnostic rejection of the material world, (which God called good) and their rejection of the physical body (which God formed, Christ took on, and God will resurrect), is actually a rebellion against our own creatureliness. As creatures, we have a beginning and an end. We have limitations. The body can only do so much, the mind only grasps a fraction of knowledge and is hindered by bias, world view, etc. We, at times, are subject to pain,8 even death, as well as joy and even ecstasy. We are dependant creatures, certainly not infinite gods. We will live forever, indeed, sustained by God. The Gnostic rejects this, he wants to believe that there is something infinite within Him, a limitlessness.

Orthodox Christianity, on the other hand, is a return to true humanity, nothing more or less. The main key to psychological well being is to re-embrace your own God given, material/spiritual condition. You are a created being, a man, made by God. You depend on Him for every breath you take. God put you here on His earth, to glorify Him, in the midst of all of this limitation, opportunity, suffering, joy, pain, and comfort. The world is in a fallen state, but God will redeem it. We don't create our own reality. We aren't God. We are people. God is above and we are below. God loves us and saves us. Hallelujah! When God made the earth He called it good – When God made your body He called it Good – Christ's body was resurrected, yours shall be also.

Gnostic Distortions of Christ's Person

I John 4:1-3 Beloved, believe not every spirit, but try the spirits whether they are of God: because many false prophets are gone out into the world. Hereby know ye the Spirit of God: every spirit that confesseth that Jesus Christ is come in the flesh is of God: And every spirit that confesseth not that Jesus Christ is come in the flesh is not of God: and this is that spirit of antichrist, whereof ye have heard that is should come; and even now already is it in the world.

Consider the contrast between Adam and Christ. Adam tried to reject his lowly state as a creature, a man, to grasp equality with God. (Through esoteric knowledge I might add, Adam and Eve were Gnostics). On the other hand, Jesus, the only true God, let go of His equality with God to become a man! This is why, at its root, Gnosticism rejects the incarnation. It is an offence because it moves in the opposite direction of Gnosticism. It is not the progression of; from man to God, but rather, God descending to man.

Gnosticism has generated two equally damning Christological errors. First, the error called Docetism, which is the belief that Christ didn't really come in the flesh, He only seemed to. Remember, to a Gnostic, trying to escape the flesh is the ideal. Coming in the flesh would be unworthy of God. In other words, Jesus wasn't truly a man. He never truly felt hunger, pain, rejection, or sorrow. He transcended all of that as God and only seemed to live a human life. In the Gnostic "Acts of John," John supposedly tells his disciples that Jesus was seen on the shore by James and John, first as a child, then as an older, bald headed man, and yet again as a young man, who left no footprints in the sand. When John went to feel His body, supposedly, "His substance was immaterial and incorporeal...As if it did not exist at all." The real John, the apostle, went to great effort to teach the church that the real Jesus is one that can be felt, touched and handled.

I John 1:1-4 That which was from the beginning, which we have heard, which we have seen with our eyes, which we have looked upon, and our hands have handled, of the Word of life; (For the life was manifested, and we have seen it, and bear witness, and show unto you that eternal life, which was with the Father, and was manifested unto us;) That which we have seen and heard declare we unto you, that ye also may have fellowship with us: and truly our fellowship is with the Father, and with his Son Jesus Christ. And these things write we unto you, that your joy may be full.

He is the one who has come and remains in the flesh. The Jesus that is coming to so many now in dreams and visions is not the Jesus of the Bible, he is the Gnostic Jesus. The real Jesus said,

"Handle me, a spirit hath not flesh and bones as you see me have." The world of the Gnostic is not the real world, it is the mystical, specious, spiritualized world. The excessive allegorization of scripture is a gnostic denial of Jesus in the flesh. For example, "The Lord said to my Lord, sit at my right hand till I make my enemies thy footstool." Psalm 110:1 is now being reinterpreted. The current idea is that Jesus is waiting for us, the militant church, to make His enemies His footstool.

Jesus Christ as the first fruit of the kingdom began the work of conquering death on an individual basis, but we, as His church will be the one to complete the task. Jesus said, (Matt 28:18), all power is given unto me in heaven and in earth, and the church today has that same power. Death will not be conquered by Jesus returning to the earth. It will be conquered when the church stands up boldly and says, "We have dominion over the earth!" How else will God be able to show Satan a people for whom death holds no fear, over whom death no longer has any power? When God can do that, Satan's hold on us will be broken forever![9]

Modern Gnostics like Earl Paulk, whom I have quoted above, would do two things, exalt the church (man) and denigrate Christ (God). In the quote above it is the church that is completing the job that Jesus started, the subjugation of death, and death won't be finally defeated at the return of Christ, it will only be defeated when we rise up and say... Gnostics spiritualize the return of Christ, they despise the thought of a literal flesh and bone Christ returning in literal clouds to rescue His elect.

A true Christology needs to be emphasized again. The church needs to worship the one who came and remains in the flesh, who didn't transcend the real world, or escape it. He fully tasted it all! Death, pain, suffering, sorrow, as well as joy, love, human touch, good food. Jesus is God with us, fully identifying with the human condition, to redeem us. After his resurrection, He didn't appear to them in a cloud, singing weird hymns, He cooked them breakfast by the shore! A docetic, spiritualized Christ awakens no compassion. In the 2nd century, Ignatius of Antioch wrote of the Gnostics,

They have no concern for love, none for the widow, the orphans, and the

afflicted, the prisoner, the hungry, the thirsty. They stay away from the eucharist, and prayer.[10]

Christian compassion springs from the good news of the one who came to suffer, (passion), with us (com), compassion. The Jesus who is coming back again, will not be some allegorical, mystical, revival within our hearts, He will be the one who has scars on His hands and feet and will touch down on the Mount of Olives, a geographical location! No one will have to say – Lo, there is Christ! All will know.

Another modern version of Docetism, is the image of the victorious Christ, the man of faith, who was always in control, never got sick, was not poor, went first class everywhere, at least one charlatan even contends that He wore designer clothes! (You know, the seamless robe!) The idea is that if you have faith, you too can transcend the reality of human life in a fallen world, your life will be a series of unbroken victories and successes. If it's not, then you must not have faith. Any compassion that comes from that view is bound to be condescending.

Jesus' life was not a series of unbroken victories and successes. He was despised and rejected of men, remember? He didn't convert everyone He appealed to, nor did He heal everyone he wanted to. He entered into complete human experience and fully tasted it. The victory of Christ over all, was through death and weakness, not success and confidence. This Gnostic generation needs to believe this!

II Corinthians 13:4 *For though he was crucified through weakness, yet he liveth by the power of God. For we also are weak in him, but we shall live with him by the power of God toward you.*

Another Gnostic Distortion of Christ

If Gnostics can't make Christ into someone who is other than human, then they try to make Him less than God. The idea is; Jesus spoke to the storm and it obeyed Him. What do we get out of this testimony? The Gnostic revelation would emphasize the word "spoke." When you receive the "Word of Faith" Gnosis, you'll see that you can speak to the storms of life also, and they will obey you! Jesus' life and works are things we can attain to, through the Gnosis. One modern Gnostic says, "The Believer is as much an incarnation as Jesus of Nazareth was."[11]

The idea that the church is as much Christ as Christ is amounts to a denial of the deity of Christ. Through our "Revelation" of "Who we are in Christ," and our "rights and privileges in Christ," we have a faith that still leaves us at the center. Using the earlier example, it's not that Jesus spoke to the storm, it's that **JESUS** spoke to the storm! We are not Jesus, nor will we ever be, He is the "monogenes" of God, the only unique Son.

Even though we are the sons of God by adoption, He is the only unique son. There is no one else like Him! To put us on a par of equality with Him is to diminish Him. Yes, we are the body of Christ, but He is Christ, not us. It is Christ who has put down Satan, and will bring all rule, power, and dominion under the authority of God. Let us exalt Jesus, who lived as 100% man and has existed always as the true God and who is worshipped above all, forever.

Is There a Remedy for Gnosticism?

Certainly, I would like to end this section with what I consider to be the ingredients of the remedy, which the church has employed before to suppress this demonic doctrine. As I said at the start, Gnosticism is not new, it's the old, repackaged, and reheated lie from the garden.

1. Teach sound doctrine.

The Gnostic climate is greatly enhanced by the impatience with doctrine that God's people presently exhibit. "The time has come when they will not endure sound doctrine." Pastors, take the time to teach the great doctrines of grace, faith, God and His attributes, the atonement, the ten commandments, etc. Especially assure the flock once again, that our God is a sovereign God, that He is the center that all else revolves around. Don't let people think that God exists for them, assure them that we were created and now exist for His pleasure! Of all doctrines, the American Pentecostal church needs a good dose of the sovereignty of God, who is blessed forever!

Along with the sovereignty of God, preach and teach the saving acts of God in history. The Gnostics make much of the knowledge of God, but their knowledge of God is entirely subjective. How is it that we know God? God has acted in history, He has cared, intervened. I believe that, and enter into a relationship with Him. I don't need a mystical experience of the cross, God has acted. Whether I feel God's love for me at a particular moment or not is almost irrelevant. God has loved me, commending His love to me by sending His Son to die on the cross. To me the question is not does God love me? But rather, have I responded to God's love, which He demonstrated in history, when Christ died.

We need to get away from those who allegorize all of scripture. Indeed, there are parables and allegories in scripture, but the Gnostics would allegorize everything, leaving us at the mercy of their subjective interpretation. David and Goliath don't have to represent any concept, they are actual people in history! It happened, God gave David victory. The manchild who would rule the nations in Revelation 12, is Jesus Christ, not us. The best interpreter of scripture is not dreams, visions, or revelations, but rather, the rest of scripture.

2. Return to the communion of the church.

God has called us to Koinonea. The promises of God can only be realized in Koinonea. It is in the community of God, that I grow in grace and in the knowledge of Him, because He comes to me and washes my feet through the brotherhood. I have not been called to wash my own feet, to be self-sufficient. The burden of trying to be super Christian has been lifted. An accountability to the community of God enables me to run the race both with patience, and untangle the obstacles, that usually hinder me.

Hebrews 12:1 *Wherefore seeing we also are compassed about with so great a cloud of witnesses, let us lay aside every weight, and the sin which doth so easily beset us, and let us run with patience the* *race that is set before us. Looking unto Jesus the author and finisher of our faith; who for the joy that was set before him endured the cross, despising the shame, and is set down at the right hand of God.*

One expression of this return, would be the return to the sacraments. In our reaction against liturgical deadness, we Gnostically almost avoid any sacrament. Gnostics didn't like the bread and wine, nor baptismal water, because those were mere earthly symbols of the spiritual reality. Jesus ordained the sacraments, to humble us and tie our spirituality to this practical, physical world, in which He came, in the flesh. There is a powerful binding affect in the communion, it has to be a sharing, breaking the bread, drinking the cup, in remembrance of Him. Form isn't evil, it's actually humbling, even the confession of the Apostles Creed would do some congregations some good.

3. Give the church a view for the long haul, an eternal perspective.

Are we looking for the instant solution, **the escape**? Or are we on a pilgrimage? Are we trying to salvage this world, and make it a better place, or do we long for heaven?

One of the major problems with Charismatic/Pentecostal perspective today is the almost complete lack of a heavenly vision. We have failed to comprehend that God's view of this world is uncompromising, it is under judgement and it is doomed. We still want to change the world. Therefore we are not on a pilgrimage through the world, willing to suffer the hostility and opposition of it. Nor are we willing to submit to the church discipline and commitment that it takes to walk through it together. We are very much trying to make it our home, by salvaging it and attempting to spiritualize it. Heaven is not the immediate hope of too many Christians. This needs to be remedied, to cure the short range, worldly, low tolerance of suffering threshold of the present church. "Too heavenly minded to be any earthly good", seems to be a valid fear of many in the church. They seem to forget that the only ones who ever actually were "earthly good" were the heavenly minded ones. Heaven needs to be preached again, this life needs to be put in its right perspective, as temporary, a testing time, shortlived, not the ultimate.

4. Direct contact needs to be established with the poor and needy.

James 1:27 Pure religion and undefiled before God and the Father is this, to visit the fatherless and widows in their affliction, and to keep himself unspotted from the world.

This is a great cure for the twin evils of Gnosticism and Secularism. Gnosticism, the exclusive desire to escape this world, "Keep yourself unspotted", is often counter-balanced with plain old involvement in others lives. Amazingly, development of your personal prayer life, and knowledge of scripture are not ends in and of themselves. The great goals for life are two, both found in this statement, "Love God supremely and love your neighbour equally." You can not keep one commandment at the expense of the other. Gnosticism seeks to shut everything else out and discover God in self. Secularism seeks to serve man, but neglects God. Balanced Orthodox Christianity is always worshipping God, a God who is "out there", not within, who can be known through His own objective self revelation, a God who has acted and is acting in history, calling a people out, unto Himself. But at the same time, Orthodox Christianity demands compassion and love of neighbour. This even goes beyond evangelizing. We aren't even told to "evangelize our neighbour", but to love our neighbour. Of course if you love some one, you will want to see them saved. But whether any one is saved or not they have value and deserve to be treated with dignity and respect. Value doesn't come to a person upon salvation, people are valuable because they are made in the image of God. God's people are witnesses to this. Gnostics valued only those they considered "chosen", the rest were the unenlightened.

There is no remedy like actually loving, serving people to bring us into the real world, the world as it is since the fall, the people that God loves and wants to redeem. People don't need to jump through

173

our hoop, in order for us to value them. Get to know them and even allow them to give us that cup of cold water. As Jesus came in the flesh, we must bring our spiritual warfare out of the cosmic heavenly realm, into the flesh and blood world of human need and interaction.

James 2:1-13 My brethren, have not the faith of our Lord Jesus Christ, the Lord of glory, with respect of persons. For if there come unto your assembly a man with a gold ring, in goodly apparel, and there come in also a poor man in vile raiment; and ye have respect to him that weareth the gay clothing, and say unto him, Sit thou here in a good place; and say to the poor, Stand thou there, or sit here under my footstool. Are ye not then partial in yourselves, and are become judges of evil thoughts? Hearken, my beloved brethren, hath not God chosen the poor of this world rich in faith, and heirs of the kingdom which he hath promised to them that love him? But ye have despised the poor. Do not rich men oppress you, and draw you before the judgement seats? Do not they blaspheme that worthy name by the which ye are called? If ye fulfil the royal law according to the scripture, Thou shalt love thy neighbour as thyself, ye do well. But if ye have respect to persons, ye commit sin, and are convinced of the law as transgressors. For whosoever shall keep the whole law, and yet offend in one point, he is guilty of all. For he that said, do not commit adultery, said also, do not kill. Now if thou commit no adultery, yet if thou kill, thou art become a transgressor of the law. So speak ye, and so do, as they that shall be judged by the law of liberty. For he shall have judgement without mercy, that hath showed no mercy; and mercy rejoiceth against judgement.

I will close with a classic description of error by Irenaeus who wrote the book, **Against Heresies**, in the early church, as an antidote against Gnosticism.

Error, indeed, is never set forth in its naked deformity, lest being thus exposed, it should at once be detected. But it is craftily decked out in an attractive dress, so as, by its outward form, to make it appear to the inexperienced ... more true than the truth itself.

As Lee said in the closing of his book, **Against the Protestant Gnostics**;

> There will be no shortcuts. If these distinctions are to be explained, in Irenaeus' words, 'To all those with whom thou art connected', that they might 'avoid such an abyss of madness and of blasphemy against Christ', then study, debate, discipline, devotion, prayer, and fasting will be required.
>
> In denying the false claims of Gnostic faith it will be necessary to confess with Irenaeus that, 'Perfect knowledge cannot be attained in this present life. Many questions must be submissively left in the hands of God.' That statement itself could serve as a concise warning to North American Protestants. For our religious expectations have been too high; our claims of religious prowess have been too great. We have failed to regard the distance between the temporal and eternal, between what we know and what there is to know.[12]

To this I say, Amen. The Grace of Our Lord Jesus Christ be with you always.

Appendix Four References

1. Kenneth Copeland Ministries, Cassette Tape #02-0028, "The Force of Love." Kenneth Copeland.
2. Ibid.
3. Kenneth Copeland. "The Believer's Voice of Victory" Broadcast.
4. "Praise the Lord" Broadcast on Trinity Broadcasting Network. July 7, 1986.
5. **Against the Protestant Gnostics.** Phillip Lee. Oxford Press. Page 27.
6. **The Road Less Travelled.** M. Scott Peck.
7. **The Agony of Deceit.** Michael Horton. Moody Press. Appendix C. Page 268.
8. Mind science cults like Christian Science, which are forms of Gnosticism, try to cope with this by denying the reality of anything evil or negative, like pain and suffering. To them, it is all an illusion. Once again, Gnosticism is the religion of escape from material reality, not a pilgrimage through it.
9. Earl Paulk. **The Proper Function of the Church.** Atlanta. K Dimension Publishers. Page 13.
10. Against the Protestant Gnostics. Phillip Lee. Oxford Press. Page 52.
11. **The Word of Faith.** Kenneth Hagin. Dec 1980.
12. **Against the Protestant Gnostics.** Phillip Lee. Oxford Press. Page 283.